EPHESIANS

God's Great Mystery Revealed
Leader / Facilitator Guide

Beholding-Is-Becoming Bible Study Series

Nancy W. Carroll

Nancy W. Carroll © 2021 All rights reserved

Donelson Press, Nashville, Tennessee.

ISBN: 978-1-944066-42-0

Library of Congress Control Number: 2021938967

Printed in the United States

Table of Contents

BEHOLDING-IS-BECOMING BIBLE STUDY SERIES

Connecting People to Jesus Christ through Scripture and Community

by

Nancy W. Carroll

www.nancywcarroll.com

His-Story/Your Story: Seeing Scripture's Big Story and Your Part in It (11 weeks)
Sweeping overview of Scripture weaving together the themes of our redemption in Jesus Christ, God's covenant to his people, and God's Kingdom now and to come.

Beholding is Becoming: Your Story in His-Story (11 weeks)
Study combining daily study of God's attributes, worship through beloved hymns, and the opportunity for participants in small group setting to tell and behold each other's stories and affirm their place in God's Big Story. Part 2 of His Story/Your Story.

Genesis: From Glory to Grace: Blessed by Our Covenant God (15 weeks)

Romans: From Grace to Glory: Gripped by the Gospel (22 weeks)

II Corinthians: Relishing and Radiating Christ in Our Cracked Lives (12 weeks)

Ephesians: God's Great Mystery Revealed: In Christ, In His Church (11 weeks)

Philippians: Advancing the Gospel Together through Our Joy in Jesus (12 weeks)

Come to Me: Finding Soul Rest in a Weary World (11 weeks)
Study giving a fresh look at beloved spiritual disciplines as invitations from Jesus Christ.

Recalibrating: Finding Our Way Home in a Disorienting World (8 weeks)
Study on Jesus' farewell address in John 13-17.

An Overflowing Life: Living Out the Inflowing Life of Christ (10 weeks)
Gospel refresher course

Dear Leaders and Facilitators:

This guide supplements the Bible study workbook *Ephesians: God's Great Mystery Revealed: In Christ, In His Church.* It gives you ideas on engaging with Scripture, guidelines on leading and being part of a small group, and teaching notes and illustrations as you study the book of Ephesians together.

The Beholding-is-Becoming Bible Study Series

There are no formulas to the Christian life, only God's grace and mystery. But we can experience the promise of his supernatural transformation in our lives.

The title for the Bible studies I've developed is found in 2 Corinthians where Paul says that as we behold him, we become more and more like him.

And we all, with unveiled face, beholding the glory of the Lord, are being transformed into the same image from one degree of glory to another. For this comes from the Lord who is the Spirit. 2 Cor 3:18 ESV

Nothing between us and God, our faces shining with the brightness of his face. And so we are transfigured much like the Messiah, our lives gradually becoming brighter and more beautiful as God enters our lives and we become like him. 2 Corinthians 3:18 The Message

One of the ways we behold him is through his Word. Although there are no guaranteed formulas, I've seen God work more than we can imagine or conceive when the following ingredients combine:

Holy Scriptures + Holy Spirit + God's Holy People + Prayer = More Than We Can Dream

God can do anything, you know—far more than you could ever imagine or guess or request in your wildest dreams! He does it not by pushing us around but by working within us, his Spirit deeply and gently within us. Ephesians 3:20 The Message

The Beholding-Is-Becoming Bible studies allow people with different learning styles to approach Scripture in different ways and in the different seasons of their lives.

Personal study/devotion time

The weekly lessons have been structured to help people learn how to read and apply Scripture to their lives and for the Kingdom. The daily questions usually take less than 10 minutes. The head/heart/hands approach encourages people to engage Scripture with their whole beings: minds, emotions, and actions. For those who chafe under directed questions, the "personal discovery sheet" provides a way to imbed the Scripture into their lives on their own. There is an express version for those overwhelmed with life which allows them to still be in Scripture a few minutes a day or a simple way to catch up on the study if they've missed a few days. The study encourages folks to read and soak in the primary source (the Bible) first, before going to commentary or teaching on those verses.

Facilitating Small Groups

Scripture comes alive as people study in community and learn from and pray for one another based on the Scriptures they are studying.

A key to developing safe and strong community is the preparation of the teacher and small group facilitators. Optimally, these leaders prepare through retreats (to begin experiencing that kind of fellowship) and weekly training to know how to best shepherd, pray for, and facilitate their groups. This guide includes simple principles for leading small groups. "The Ten Commandments for Being in a Small Group" can be copied and handed out as you begin the study.

Teaching

This guide gives resources to help those teaching Ephesians. Teaching notes, illustrations, and suggested movie clips are provided to help give emotional connection to the Scriptural content and fill in the handouts provided in the commentary section of the Ephesians study.

Commentary

The commentary supplements personal study and gives people thoughts from theologians. A bibliography of these commentaries is also included in the Ephesians workbook.

My Prayers for the Beholding-Is-Becoming Studies

- ✦ For people to behold God in Scripture and become more like him.
- ✦ For Jesus Christ to be seen as the thread and theme through all of Scripture.
- ✦ For people to develop the habit of engaging with Scripture on a daily basis.
- ✦ For people to gain confidence in studying Scripture on their own.
- ✦ For people to experience learning and living out Scripture in community.
- ✦ For people to learn to be biblical thinkers.

I pray that you become more like him as you behold him and that you find a safe and strong community to walk with you as you meditate on his Word.

In Christ,

Nancy W. Carroll

P.S. If you have questions or would like information on these studies or leaders' retreats, please contact me at nancy@nancywcarroll.com.

General Principles of Facilitating a Small Bible Study Group

Pray

Remember we live in an enchanted universe. This is God's supernatural work. It is not up to you. Keep in dialog with God and remember He is in control and He will love and lead through you. Pray before and during your time of leading and facilitating. You will need him and he will show up. Pray for your own heart to be most gripped by the gospel; for each of the people in your group to behold and become like him; and for revival.

Love and Respect

Shepherding people in a small group will be harder and better than you think. God will have to love through you because it won't always be easy on your own to love all the people all the time. Love them right where they are at and where God is taking them. Pray that you will "see" them well. There may be no better gift than for someone to take the time to see you well and affirm who you are in Jesus Christ. Respect their time, their thoughts, and God's Word and work in their lives. Don't pressure or shame those who come unprepared but pray that they will begin to become so hungry for God's Word that they will find the time to engage with Scripture and the study. It is comforting to be part of a group where they know that there is balanced sharing of God's Word and that it is safe to share their hearts and that the leader can gently keep the group's goals met (sharing Scripture and their lives) in the promised time frame.

Prepare

- Pray.
- Do your lesson (answering the questions).
- Complete Personal Discovery Sheet.
- Highlight your lesson with introductory statement, noting key questions, thinking through time management, considering how to engage those who are quiet.
- Follow up with the individuals in your group during the week (especially if they shared a heart request or are struggling with the study/Scripture, or if they are quiet or are not sharing any requests). This can be done through phone, text, email, or in your natural connections during the week.

And to the perfectionists out there who worry they're never totally prepared or feel like they've failed:

Dance the gospel three-step waltz. Repent. Believe. Fight. (This waltz analogy is thanks to Dr. Bob Flayhart, senior pastor, Oak Mountain Presbyterian Church in Birmingham, Alabama.)

Repent: We're never really ready. We can never be enough. We will fail. It's okay.

Believe: God already knew. He is pleased that we are available. He is more powerful than we can imagine. He loves those in our group more than we do.

Fight: Because we have such a high view of God, his Word and the people in our groups, we will be humble about our mistakes and not quit. We will keep learning and spend the time to be as prepared as possible to lead our groups.

"Wing Men / Wing Women"

Group size in Bible studies can vary from two to 20+ people. If possible, when facilitating a larger group, it's helpful to find a co-leader. This allows you to prepare together, pray for your group, share the facilitator role, redirect conversation going in the wrong direction, and be there if one of you has an emergency or can't make it to the group time.

The Get REAL Club!

We long for **real**-ationships: with God, our spouses, families, friends, and work/classmates. Our God is a relational, redemptive God who through Jesus Christ seeks us out for the ultimate Abba Father/ beloved child relationship. This study gives an opportunity to be real and connect with a smaller group.

Thank you for your willingness to enter into other people's lives and facilitate a small group. It is a great privilege and responsibility ("response-ability"). You will be surprised how God enters into your own life as you trust him in walking out Christ's command in Matthew 10:8: "Freely you have received, freely give."

Here are some simple principles to think of as you begin connecting with your small group members in a "REAL" way.

R   Be real! Be vulnerable. Let group members see the real you. (Scary, huh!)
          Respect: Their time, confidences, privacy, relationships.

E   Encourage with Christ and Scripture.
          Envelop with prayer.
          Envision what they can be in Christ.

A   Available: Being fully present to others is a gift.
          Approachable: By letting them see the real you, they'll feel safe around you.

L   Look. See them as Christ sees them.
          Listen. With your heart. Don't interrupt but follow up with questions of curiosity.
          Love with Christ's love

Ten Commandments for Leading a Small Group

Thou Shalt Remember

The Lord Thy God is in control, loves thee, calls (John 15:16) and enables thee (I Thes. 5:24) and will never leave nor forsake thee (Joshua 1:5-6). God is at work through his Holy Word, Holy Spirit and holy people. Thou shalt "feel" like thee fail or blow it many times, but God is always pleased with thee in Christ Jesus.

Thou Shalt Respect

The Word of God and its supernatural power to work in lives
Time: Starteth on time. Endeth on time.
Each person in thine group, personality, point of view, and story. Each one (including thee!) carries pains, fears, sin habits, struggles, insecurities, quirks.
Thine families and friends. Don't allow people to share about others what they will later regret.
Confidentiality: What is shared in the group stays in the group unless given permission.

Thou Shalt Realize the Privilege and the Sacrifice

'Tis a great privilege to walk with other people in Scripture and significant aspects of their hearts and lives. It requireth a sacrifice of time, agenda, heart, and resources. 'Twill be harder and better than thou anticipate. Thou shalt be prepared by praying, studying, and knowing thine role.

Thou Shalt Keep Focused

Keepeth thine group on topic gently. Be present and actively listen. Eliminate distractions such as cell phones, texting, side conversations, interruptions.

Thou Shalt Repent of Fixing

'Tis not the place to fix nor giveth advice; 'tis the place to listen and to focus on God's Word and encourage thine group to be honest. People wanteth a place of safety and strength where they are listened to and reminded of the gospel and pointed to Christ and Scripture.

Thou Shalt Handle with Care

Thou shalt not gossip nor judge nor correct bad theology. We are all broken people in a broken world. Prayeth that God givest thee a supernatural love for each person in thine group (because some perhaps won't be "naturally" loveable).

Thou Shalt Be Patient

There will not be instant chemistry. 'Twill taketh time to build trust and connect with each other.

Thou Shalt Connect

Thou shalt pray for and connect with each individual in thine group. Be creative.
This can be done via email, phone, text, hallway moments, getting together, etc.

Thou Shalt Pause

Thou must be comfortable with silence. Thou may prepare quieter members that thou will ask them questions after the first few weeks. Thou may need to solicit the help of more talkative members to also pause for quieter ones to answer. Encourage through short, validating words that you've heard them.

Thou Shalt Pray

Pray without ceasing. Pray before, during, after. Pray for and with the members in thine group. Pray for God to be glorified, for us to remember Christ, and to leave with hope.

Ten Commandments for Being in a Small Group

Thou Shalt Remember

The Lord Thy God is sovereign over what group thou are in and who thine leader is. He loves thee and will never leave nor forsake thee (Joshua 1:5-6). Remember that God worketh through His Holy Word, Holy Spirit, and holy people. Remember that it feeleth somewhat uncomfortable and artificial for everyone, especially in the beginning (see *Thou Shalt Be Patient* below.)

Thou Shalt Respect

The Word of God and its supernatural living power to work in lives. If you haven't had time to do your lesson, listen more, share less.

Time: Come on time. End on time. Groups begin dissolving if they can't keep to the time limits.

Each person *in thine group*, personality and point of view and story. Everyone has pains, fears, sin habits, struggles, insecurities.

Thine families and friends. Don't share anything about anyone that you may regret later.

Confidentiality: What is shared in the group stays in the group unless given permission.

Thou Shalt Be Prepared and Participate

Thou hast made a commitment to be in Scripture and walk with others in some of the significant aspects of their hearts and lives. 'Tis a privilege. Trust God that He will give thee time for preparation and courage to share and faith that thou will receive and be transformed.

Thou Shalt Keep Focused

Keep on topic. Actively listen. Eliminate distractions. Turneth off cell phones. Don't text or start side conversations or interrupt others while they are sharing.

Thou Shalt Repent of Fixing

'Tis not the place to fix nor give advice. 'Tis a place to listen and to focus on God's Word and be honest. We all long for a place of safety and strength where we are listened to and reminded of the gospel and pointed to Christ and Scripture.

Thou Shalt Handle with Care

Thou shalt not gossip or judge or correct. We're all broken people in a broken world. Pray that God will give thee a supernatural love for each person in your group.

Thou Shalt Be Patient

There will not be instant chemistry and it will take time to build trust and connect with each other.

Thou Shalt Connect

Thou shalt pray for and connect with the other members in your group. In some groups, 'tis essential to wear nametags if only for the sake of the swiss-cheese brained among thee.

Thou Shalt Pause

For thou who love to leapeth into each conversation and answereth each question, train thyself to pause to give non-leapers a chance to muster the courage to answer or share. Encourage others by actively listening and validating their responses through nods.

Thou Shalt Pray

Pray without ceasing for thyself and thine group, thine leader and thine teacher and for the glory of our Triune God. Share real requests with thine group members and remember to pray for each other throughout the week.

PERSONAL DISCOVERY SHEET

At the end of each weekly lesson, you are invited to complete a Personal Discovery Sheet. This gives you a way to approach a specific section of Scripture in what I call an "hour-glass" method. You begin broadly by listing the content or verses. Narrow it down to two to four main thoughts. Then funnel it all into a short sentence give the main subject of the verses you are studying. Then widen back out to state the aim of the author for that passage and how to phrase that in a question. Finally, in the final section broaden to apply the passage to your life.

This discovery sheet is adapted from training at Bible Study Fellowship and Beeson Divinity School. I'm thankful to Bob Flayhart for learning to apply the Scriptures in a gospel three-step waltz of repent, believe, and fight.

This approach often appeals to those who love word puzzles or, like me, are scattered and need a framework to help them organize their thoughts.

This discovery sheet also helps prepare you to teach by narrowing in on the main themes and applications of a specific passage of Scripture. I've found it's wonderful when a group shares the results of their personal discovery sheets. It reveals how the Holy Spirit uses all of us together to communicate and apply his living Word.

Below is a brief description for each section. The following page is a sample from Ephesians 3:14-21.

Personal Discovery Sheet

Bible Verses

CONTENT

Read the passage enough times to be comfortable with contents. List the content by verse or larger section. This is usually between five to twenty concepts based on how many verses you're reading. Look for repeated phrases or words that seem to characterize the passage and include them in your list. Underline, circle, or emphasize words that seem to be the most important.

DIVISIONS

Divide the content into two to four main "thoughts." Use a sentence as a heading for each division. Write the verses down for each division.

ESSENCE OF PASSAGE

Using the divisions from the passage, write a ten-word or less subject sentence that gives you the thrust of the passage. Ask yourself, "What is this passage about?" Ideally, the subject sentence should be specific enough that you would be able to locate it in the Bible.

ESSENTIAL QUESTION/AIM

The aim is the main transformational truth you want to learn, remember, or do after reading this Scripture. It may be just for yourself or include others. Ask yourself, "What do I want to remember and live by after reading this passage?" Your aim should be short and definite and should point to the hope of what God and his grace can do in and through you for his glory, not what you're going to "try harder" to do for him. Putting it in a form of a question helps to link it to applications.

APPLICATIONS

Write specific questions or challenges based on your essential aim/question and from the divisions. Are there specific areas in which you need to repent? To believe God and his Word? To live out and apply the gospel? To see and rely on Christ? To have or communicate hope?

EXAMPLE OF PERSONAL DISCOVERY SHEET

Ephesians 2:1-10

CONTENT

2:1-2: You were **dead** in trespasses, sin in which you walked, following the world, prince of power of air, spirit at work, sons of disobedience

2:3: in which **we all lived** in passions of our flesh, desires of our body, mind, **by nature children of wrath** like rest of mankind

2:4-5 **BUT GOD**, rich in mercy, great love for us, when dead in trespasses, made us alive together with Christ. **By grace you have been saved**.

2:6: Raised us up, seated us with him in heavenly places **in Christ**

2:7: To show immeasurable **riches of his grace in kindness** to us in Christ Jesus

2:8-9: For **by grace through faith** you have been saved, **not of own doing**, gift of God, not works so no one may boast

2:10: We are **his workmanship created in Christ Jesus for good works** which God prepared beforehand that we should walk in them.

DIVISIONS

2:1-3 But You: Paul shows who we were without Christ.

2:4-7 But God: Paul describes God's mercy, love, and grace in making us alive together with Christ.

2:8-10 By Grace: Paul shows how and why God saved us and who we are now.

ESSENCE OF PASSAGE

God saves us by grace to purpose-filled life in Christ.

ESSENTIAL QUESTION/AIM

Question: What part of these truths are most difficult for you to believe (who you were, God's great love in saving you, who you are called to be now) and why?

Aim: To recapture the wonder of what God did for us and why he did it.

APPLICATIONS

Do I remember who I was? What is my response for those who are the "walking dead" now?

How have I dealt with the "humility" of having nothing to do with my salvation? No credit?

Where do I need to hear "BUT GOD" in a current "dead" situation in my life?

How can my life display God's riches of grace in kindness to my world today?

What work has God prepared for me to do? What does it mean to "walk" in that work?

If I believed I was his masterpiece instead of a "piece of work" how would that change me?

Bibliography and Teaching Resources

Chapell, Bryan. *Ephesians: Reformed Expository Commentary* (Phillipsburg, NJ: P&R Publishing, 2009).

Crabb, Larry. *66 Love Letters: A Conversation with God that Invites You into His Story* (Nashville, Tenn.: Thomas Nelson, 2009).

ESV Study Bible, English Standard Edition (Wheaton, Ill.: Crossway Bible, 2008).

Fernando, Ajith. *The Fullness of Christ: Ephesians* (London: Authentic Media, 2007).

Hughes, R. Kent. *Ephesians: The Mystery of the Body of Christ,* Preaching the Word Series (Wheaton, Ill: Crossway Books, 1990).

Lee-Thorpe, Karen, ed. *Ephesians, Life Change Series* (Colorado Springs, Co.: NavPress, 1985).

Life Application Bible (Grand Rapids, Mich.: Zondervan Publishing House and Wheaton, Ill.: Tyndale House Publishers, 1991).

Mears, Henrietta C. *What the Bible is All About* (Ventura, Calif.: Regal Books, 1953).

The NIV Serendipity Bible for Study Groups (Grand Rapids, Mich.: Zondervan Bible Publishers, 1988).

O'Brien, Peter T. *The Letter to the Ephesians* (Grand Rapids: Eerdmans Publishing, 1999).

Peterson, Eugene H. *The Message* (Colorado Springs, Co.: NavPress, 1993).

Stott, John R. W. *Ephesians: Building a Community in Christ* (Downers Grove, Ill: InterVarsity Press, 1998).

Stott, John R. W. *The Message of Ephesians* (Downers Grove, Ill: InterVarsity Press, 1979).

Thielman, Frank. *Exegesis of Ephesians.* Greek Exegetical Class. (Birmingham: Beeson Divinity School, 2007).

Thielman, Frank. *Theology of the New Testament* (Grand Rapids, Mich. Zondervan, 2005).

Teaching Notes

The Ephesians Bible Study is divided into two sections: Weekly Lessons and Teaching Notes / Commentary. The goal is for people to engage with Scripture on their own first and then supplement with teaching and commentary.

This section on teaching notes will help fill in the weekly teaching handouts found in the commentary section.

Week 1: *Discover Your Destiny*
Overview of Ephesians

It's in Christ that we find out who we are and what we are living for.
Ephesians 1:11 The Message

All progress in spiritual life comes by understanding a truth which is already true.
It is not something that God is going to do, but something he has already done.
Therefore, it is available to you the minute you understand it and grasp it.
Ray Stedman

Ephesians reveals the riches of who you are in Christ and what He has planned for you and the Church. What do you want God to help you believe is true for you through this study?

How do you want God to apply the "already true" truths to your life?

First Week's Goal:
Give opportunity for group to connect, learn a bit about each other, and get them excited about the study of Ephesians.

VISUAL AID: Bring jigsaw puzzle. Spread out in front of group.
Does your life ever feel like a mess, like this puzzle, and you've lost the box so you don't even know what the picture is supposed to look like? There are probably pieces missing. You're overwhelmed. Why even start?

Pick up piece.
Different shapes, different colors, yet all fit together to form a picture. Ask them to pick a piece they may identify with and ask why. Is it color? Lots of edges? Complex? Solid color?

Go around circle and ask:

- Name, family/work
- Why did you pick up this piece?
- If you know how you would "fit" what kind of puzzle piece would you be?
- Why taking Ephesians?

Why study Ephesians?
First question, why study the Bible? The Bible gives you a hint at the finished picture of your life. What the story is all about. That it is all worth it. Most importantly, it reveals Christ. It reveals you.

In his epistle to the Romans, Paul lays out the gospel like a lawyer in a courtroom. In 2 Corinthians, he is the very real and weak minister of the gospel laying out his life. In Ephesians, Paul is a symphony director who uses Spirit-inspired words to let believers hear the beautiful song of the gospel so they will know who they are in Christ, what God has done for them, and what he has planned for them. John Mackay, former president of Princeton Theological Seminary in reference to Ephesians, wrote "This letter is pure music. . .What we read here is truth that sings, doctrine set to music."

Has the glorious music of the gospel faded in your life?
Ephesians resets the "radio dial" so you clearly hear what God has done for you. Ephesians is a gospel "GPS" always recalibrating you to show who you are IN Christ and encouraging you to believe it. It includes beautiful prayers that you will grasp his love for you, and it takes you by the hand like a dearly loved child to walk out in love who you really are. God reveals his great mystery that we walk hand-in-hand with other believers as the church to display the glory of God in Jesus Christ.

We're studying Ephesians to recover the music of the gospel for our souls and sing and play our individual instruments together so the world will hear the gospel in symphony. **In Ephesians you will discover your destiny, to recognize that you are a "master-piece" in the puzzle which will reveal the grace and glory of Jesus Christ.**

I. Background of Ephesians — Eph. 1:1-2

Author: Paul. Apostle of Christ Jesus by the will of God.
<u>Apostle:</u> Specially chosen, called and sent one, with authority to teach, by the will of God.

(Read Acts for more information on Paul.) Paul always knew it was by God's grace, nothing to do with his efforts. Originally called Saul. Jew's Jew. Pharisee's pharisee. Saul was disgusted by this new cult. He was a man with a mission to wipe these Christ followers out. A man you couldn't imagine turning to your side. God zapped this man. The resurrected Jesus met and blinded him. Saul/Paul listened, repented, and believed.

I think he was always amazed that he was an apostle: chosen, sent especially when he considered who he had been. God let him know that his primary purpose was to go to the Gentiles. "But God, let me reach my own people. I'd be ready to do that." God sent him to first to the Gentiles and their kings (and also, to the Jews).

Paul had to battle "voices" also. Was he haunted by his pre-Christ actions? He talks about being least of all God's people. He owned this truth: God has given me the grace to speak to these people.

He reaches Ephesus on his third missionary journey. He'd been a believer for about 20 years. He probably was in his mid to late 50's. He stays there for almost three years. He writes this letter from prison in Rome 61-62 ad. Unlike some other letters, Ephesians is not addressing specific problem. It is probably meant as a circular letter to be sent to believers throughout Asia Minor. It was meant to read out loud to congregation.

Ephesians deals with who they are in Christ and what the Church is, and how to live out who they are. You've got to know who you are and what you possess to be able to "live it out without gutting it out."

Place/Time: What was Ephesus like?
Ephesus has many parallels to the city I live in, Birmingham, Alabama. It was literally the "Magic City" of its time with a bustling trade in the dark arts (Acts 19). A busy commercial port and capital of the Roman province of Asia, Ephesus was one of the largest cities in the world of Paul's time, filled with Gentiles and Jews, slaves and free, Greeks and Romans. Ephesus was especially proud of its Temple of Artemis, which was one of the Seven Wonders of the World. "Ancient accounts and continuing evidence amid the archeological ruins demonstrate that the economy and culture of the entire region were as mired in materialism, sensuality, and idolatrous diversion as any modern city." (Bryan Chapell) Paul spent three years there on his third missionary journey, teaching in synagogues and houses, discipling and planting a church. He made a major impact on the culture and economy of Ephesus (Acts 19-20).

Ephesus had a huge tourist trade. The biggest attraction was the Temple of Artemis or Diana, one of seven wonders of world. Diana was fertility goddess. This temple was the pride of the city, four times the size of the Parthenon. It held 25,000. Think in terms of money (Wall Street) or sports (Bryant Denny, Jordan-Hare, University of Michigan football stadiums) or entertainment (Hollywood or Orlando). It had a large middle-class population. Ephesus was literally a "magic city," involved with sorcery. The sons of Sceva tried to cash in on Paul's power. Paul made a negative economic impact on the city. Nothing like that to get the attention of people. but looked at what a spiritual impact Paul had on the city: Ephesian believers were convicted of not just playing church. They went to their closets, burned all their magic scrolls. In today's term it would be a $2.5 million bonfire.

Audience

Saints: holy and set apart for God. If you are a believer, you qualify as a saint.

Dual residency: in Ephesus and in Christ. It is the same for us: in Birmingham, in Christ. Are you content in where God has called you?

You are a saint, a son and daughter of the King, set apart for a purpose.

II. Purpose of Ephesians — Eph. 1: 10, 3:10

Eph 1:2 *grace and peace to you.*

These are not "toss aside" words. Key themes throughout the book:

Grace: God's total initiative on our behalf, undeserved favor and power. Grace appears 27 times in this book.

Peace: In Hebrew, shalom. It denotes wholeness, as it should be.

This is a book of reconciliation, renewed relationships, man to God, and man to man.

Peace through grace. All God's doing: in Jesus Christ.
Structure of this letter: Paul's pattern: Who you are/therefore how to live. Describes your inheritance and then how to invest it. Be/do. Theory/practice. Be/live. Note that commands don't start until chapter 4.

Purpose of Ephesians: **know who you are in Christ, how to live it out.**

What are some central themes of the book?
Two main themes of Ephesians:

Christ has reconciled all creation to himself and to God

Christ has united people from all nations to himself and to one another in his church.

The key verse is Ephesians 1:9-10 *"making known to us the mystery of his will, according to his purpose, which he set forth in Christ as a plan for the fullness of time, to unite all things in him, things in heaven and things on earth."* (All Scripture references ESV unless noted.)

Paul puts together the puzzle pieces to show God's glory in Christ, in the Church, and his lavish love and purpose for you. Be amazed as his picture emerges!

In Christ, everything will be summed up and brought together—heaven and earth, people of all nations—and it will be through his Church.

III. Your Purpose — Eph. 1-6

If you read Ephesians, you have to grapple with amazing truths: you are a son and daughter with a destiny. You have a purpose to be to the praise of his glory. You display God's grace and glory. Your puzzle piece matters. You are God's work of art, masterpiece created to showcase his grace (undeserved favor) and his glory (the weight of every facet of his being). The heavenly realms are looking at what only you can display of God's character together with the Church.

Application
Begin the battle of your mind and heart. Believe it or not. Act on it. As you face the realities of your week, I know who I am and I am discovering my destiny.

Prayer
You are his master-piece, a beautiful, unique and vital puzzle piece fit together with other believers to display the full picture of Jesus Christ to the world and heavenly realms.

Week 2: And Can It Be? (Yes!)
Ephesians 1:1-14

Note: Because of the richness of Ephesians 1:3-14, we spent two weeks soaking in these amazing truths This is Part 1.

Where are you battling to believe what's already true for you in Christ?
Back to the basics
I am overwhelmed by the truths of who God says I am in verses 1:3-14 and it exposes my unbelief. I don't think I'm not alone in my unbelief. The Holy Spirit nudged me to slow down to go back to the basics. Like a musician practicing scales, hearing each note, we will go through each concept in these amazing verses.

Visual Aid
Movie clip (all little girls are princesses) from *A Little Princess.*
https://www.youtube.com/watch?v=hoZuMb19RJ4

Sara Crewe was apple of her wealthy daddy's eye; her mother has died. Sara lived lavishly in India, father went off to WWI and Sara went to boarding school with evil Mrs. Minchin. At this point of the story, her father is presumed dead and Sara has been banned to the attic, no money, a pauper, slaving away for the other wealthy girls. (Pay special attention to the facial expressions of Mrs. Minchin.)

Mrs. Minchen: When are you going to learn that real life has nothing to do with your fantasies? It's a cruel nasty world out there and it's your duty to make the best of it. Give up your dreams and just live a productive and useful life.

Sara Crewe: I understand what you're saying. I just don't believe it.

Mrs. Minchen: Do you still fancy yourself a princess? Look around you. Why, just look in the mirror.

Sara Crewe: I am a princess. All girls are. Even if you live in an attic, even if you wear rags, even if you're not pretty or smart or young. We are all princesses. Didn't your father ever tell you that? Didn't he?

I. Prince, Princess or Pauper

Your Abba Father has called you his prince/princess—no matter how old, how pretty, how smart, what kind of attic you're living in. You have his words right here in Scripture. You have been blessed, chosen, adopted, redeemed by the blood of Jesus Christ. The Holy Spirit sealed the deal. He is flooding you with assurance in the midst of your pauper life in the attic.

Who's your daddy? Who are you going to believe?

Ephesians was my "epiphany." I was teaching Ephesians for BSF and all I could hear is my constant companion—the Lie Guy. Let me introduce him to those of you who are new to the study. (Show puppet of skunk.)

He shouts in my ear, "You are such a loser. How can you stand and teach each week when you always fail? You hypocrite! Look how you yelled at your kids this morning.

In Ephesians the Lie Guy collided with Truth Teller/Scripture.

I totally believed in my head Scripture was true as my only truth, but in my heart I was battling the Lie Guy constantly criticizing me. Who am I going to choose to believe?

People, Scripture is true. And it's true for you, not just for those around you. Even in your attics and with the Mrs. Minchens, even if you're acting like Mrs. Minchen. I want to be Sara Crewe, in the midst of the attic reality, living with the words of my father playing the song of the gospel to my heart.

All those "in Christ" are princes and princesses. Your Father has told you so and done it all for you.

II. Hear the Beauty of Each Note of Who You Are

I have a habit with my Bible. As I go through, I have a code. "P' for promises. Capital "A" for attribute of God. Lowercase "a" for attribute for me, "C" for command, "W" for warning, a triangle for Trinitarian reference. I've started putting "DD" for Done Deal. Those past tense, passive voice verses where God has said this is already done for me. Already true. I don't have to "do" anything verses. All of God's initiative before I was conceived before time began. If you go through these 14 verses, only in vs. 13 do we "do" anything and that one thing we do is to believe.

We'll go through a few of these amazing attributes/facts/notes of who we are in Christ. We'll dwell on those two amazing words "in Christ" in our third point. Next week, we will remind ourselves again and see how it all fits together in Christ and for the praise of the glory of God

But first, some individual "notes" of the scales:

Blessed/blessing: (*barak* in Hebrew, *eulogia* in Greek) It is God's first action to man in Genesis (Genesis

1:28) and central to his covenant (Genesis 12). The word means praise, consecration, invoke happiness on, heavenly joy.

Heavenly Realms: Used exclusively in Ephesians (five times), this means "the unseen world of spiritual reality." It is the already/not yet overlap of Heaven into our earthly reality.

Chosen: God selected you for himself (Greek *exelexato*) before you had anything to do with it, before the foundation of the world. It is not by chance, nor by your choice. It is not by accident, nor by your action. You are not chosen because you are already holy and blameless (without blemish), nor because he thinks you have the potential.

Holiness is a result not a basis for God's choosing.
Bryan Chapell writes, "The holiness that God requires, he also supplies not by our works, but by our union with his holy Son who shares with us his own status of holiness. . . . God sees me as being as holy as his own Son."

Predestined: (Greek *proorizo*) The simple definition for this difficult doctrine is *determined beforehand*. This is a word that Paul uses to comfort believers, not alienate outsiders. "Predestination was never meant to be a doctrinal club used to batter people into acknowledgement of God's sovereignty. Rather, the message of God's love preceding our accomplishments and outlasting our failures was meant to give us a profound sense of confidence and security in God's love so that we will not despair in situations of great difficulty, pain, and shame." (Bryan Chapell)

Adopted: The Greek word (*huiothesia*) denotes putting into position as a son, with all the rights, privileges and inheritance of a natural son.

Adoption is such a special word because our children are adopted. Do you know what it feels like to be an adoptive parent? You long for a relationship, you long to give love, not based on this child's past performance or anticipated performance. You will go to all lengths and expense to lavishly love that child. No requirements.

What do we desire for our adopted children? We hope we can show them how much they are loved, how sought after they are, how much they belong, what joy they bring us just by being our children, nothing they do. Can you believe that God loves you, his adopted son and daughter, in that way? Or do you believe the Lie Guy?

Lie Guy: Choose you? You've never been chosen for anything in your life. How disappointed God must be that you're not living up to your potential. And look at all he's done for you.

Truth Teller: Stop right now! God knows all. Therefore, he is not surprised or disappointed in you. It is his job to make you holy. He will provide for you his adopted son and daughter. He takes great pleasure in you.

Adoption: His initiative, his choice, before creation of world.

Redeemed: This word (Greek: *apolutrosis*) is from the slave market and provides a perfect picture of our hopeless and helpless condition. It means to purchase back, deliver from sin, to ransom from futility (I Pet 1:18-21).

Forgiven: Webster's defines forgiveness as to release from resentment. The Greek (*aphesis*) means a remission of sins or trespasses, deliverance and liberty, to cancel a debt or remove a penalty. God chooses to remember our sins no more (Jeremiah 31:34, Hebrews 8:12). He will never recall what he chooses not to remember.

Lavished with grace: Lavish means extravagant. In the Greek, it means to cause to abound, to make extremely rich. When you couple lavish with the riches of his grace (unmerited favor and power for you), "it makes it crystal clear that the readers' redemption is all of grace. Words are hardly adequate to describe the inexhaustible nature of God's giving." (Peter O'Brien)

Made known: God has revealed the mystery of his will to us through His Word and Spirit.

Sealed: Seal (*sphragizo*) denotes a mark of ownership, security, authenticity, and destination. In Biblical times, the stamp of a signet ring in wax over a scroll was proof of authenticity and ownership.

Guarantee: Guarantee has the same meaning as our modern term for deposit or down payment. It also means pledge, a word picture of an engagement ring as a tangible reminder of the promises ahead.

To the praise of his glory: This "beautiful phrase needs to be unpacked. The glory of God is the revelation of God, and the glory of his self-disclosure as a gracious God. To live to the praise of the glory of his grace is both to worship him ourselves by words and deeds as the gracious God he is, and to cause others to see and to praise him, too." (John Stott)

Lie Guy: Jesus paid this awful price for you and look how you're blowing it. Don't you think you could live up to his price? You loser. He might have initially forgiven you but there's got to be a limit.

Truth Teller: Stop! God so longed to be in restored relationship of a father to a son/daughter that he was willing to pay the dreadful price of the death of his only son Jesus Christ. Nothing will ever change that restored relationship. You are forever forgiven. You are forever his. You belong to God. You are worth it.

As you hear and believe (which is all you have to do in this whole passage) you are marked with a seal. You are God's possession forever. You will share in the inexhaustible inheritance. Done deal. Guaranteed. Pledged. God's possession. Nothing will change that. You are the real thing.

Lie Guy: How can it be true if you don't feel like the real thing?

Truth Teller: All you have to do is hear, believe, and be in Christ. God does it all. He is the one who marks you with a seal. Jesus bought you back.

These are not future promises, but past-tense, "passive-voice" DD (done deal) truths about you. Who are you going to believe, your Father or the Lie Guy?

III. Hear the Repeated Beat of the Melody IN Christ

In Christ! Eleven times in these verses. "In Christ" is the melodic line tying together these Scriptures, this book.

As you begin to hear the beautiful individual notes of who you are, hear the throbbing beat of "in Christ" which permeates this passage and the whole book of Ephesians. It is the very real, very mystical union believers have with their head, Jesus Christ. "All that God has done for his people, and for which he is praised, has been effected in and through Christ." (Peter O'Brien) We will play the melody of these verses again next week as we see how all of this comes together in God's purpose for the world and for us in Christ.

Remember little Sara Crewe. Her father had taught her so well that when she found herself abandoned in the attic she could look beyond her circumstances and the voices screaming at her not to be a fool. "I am a princess. Every girl who believes in Christ is a princess. It doesn't matter where you live, what you do, what you wear, what you look like, how old you are, how much you weigh. . . .in God's sight you are holy and blameless, without blemish."

We are all loved princes and princesses. Our Father has told us so.
You are God's chosen, lavishly loved adopted son and daughter. You are a prince/princess with all the rights and responsibilities of royalty. You are to the praise of his glory. You are his glorious inheritance, and you have a glorious inheritance. You are forever his. He takes great pleasure in you, not because of anything you do, but just because he is your Abba Father and you are his princess/prince.

Will you hear your Father's voice? Will you begin to hear the notes and melody of the gospel?

It may sound like a fairy tale…but it is your deepest reality IN Christ

Long, long ago he decided to adopt us into his family through Jesus Christ. (What pleasure he took in planning this!) He wanted us to enter into the celebration of his lavish gift-giving through his beloved Son. Because of the sacrifice of the Messiah, his blood poured out on the altar of the Cross, we're a free people—free of penalties and punishments chalked up by all our misdeeds. *And not just barely free, either. Abundantly free!*

He thought of everything, provided for everything we could possibly need, letting us in on the plans he took such delight in making. He set it all out before us in Christ, a long-range plan in which everything would be brought together and summed up in him, everything in deepest heaven, everything on planet earth.

It's in Christ that we find out who we are and what we are living for. **Ephesians 1:11 The Message**
Can you hear the Father as he calls you his daughter and princess? His son and prince?

Where do you need to practice your scales? Hear each note of the gospel?

Where do you need to start spending your inheritance?

Week 2B *And Can it Be? (Yes!) Part 2*
Ephesians 1:3-14

Where do you need to hear the music of the gospel to believe whose you are and who it's all for?

Note: Because of the richness of Ephesians 1:3-14, we spent two weeks soaking in these amazing truths This is Part 2.

Last week we slowed down to hear the individual notes of who we are IN Christ in Ephesians 1:3-14. This week we pull it together so you hear the repeated beat—IN Christ—and hear the chords or stanzas. Hear the refrain. Hear and sing the melody. Hear and believe!

We're going from who we are in Christ to whose we are and who it is all for.

I. Hear His Song Over You — Eph 1:3-14

Visual Aid
Movie clip of opening scene from *August Rush*. Listen to the orphan's words, the background sounds, and see how this boy believes and hears the music in the midst of the "Lie Guys" around him. https://www.youtube.com/watch?v=lZwuBuTBFYQ

Do you believe in the music of the gospel? This good news that we just read. Do you hear your Abba Father singing over you?

The Lord your God is with you, he is mighty to save. He will take great delight in you, he will quiet you with his love, he will rejoice over you with singing." Zephaniah 3:17

II. Hear the Repeated Beat: IN CHRIST

"'In Christ" is Paul's throbbing heartbeat in Ephesians and throughout his epistles. This simple phrase describes the mystical, organic union (think of John 15's visual of vine and branches) of Christ in the believer and the believer in Christ. Through this union, Christ frees us from sin's mastery over our lives and enables and compels us to good works and demonstrates his own power through us. Because believers are joined to Christ in this mystical way, they share not only his experiences but also his very identity, so that the Father looks upon believers as though they were Christ himself, accounting to them Jesus status and rights."[1] It is both positional and relational.

---

[1] "Union with Christ: What Does it Mean to Be 'in Christ'?" *Spirit of the Reformation Study Bible* (Zondervan: Grand Rapids, MI, 2003), 1900.

Every spiritual blessing is ours IN Christ and God makes it clear that Christ is his Beloved and therefore, in him, we are also the beloved of God. This union is accomplished by Christ's sacrificial redemption of us through his blood which offers us forgiveness and God's lavish grace. Our only "work" in this glorious position, power and relationship is to *believe* (Eph 1:13, John 6:29).

The Heidelberg Catechism answers this in question 60 **"How are you right with God?"**

"Only by true faith in Jesus Christ. Even though my conscience accuses me of having grievously sinned against all God's commandments and of never having kept any of them, and even though I am still inclined toward all evil, nevertheless, without my deserving it at all, out of sheer grace, God grants and credits to me the perfect satisfaction, righteousness, and holiness of Christ, as if I had never sinned nor been a sinner, as if I had been as perfectly obedient, as Christ was obedient for me. All I need to do is to accept this gift of God with a believing heart."

Now can you see why *"in Christ"* was Paul's very heartbeat? Hear, understand and believe this repeated beat.

III. Hear the Three Stanzas

a. Who's Your Daddy? — Eph 1:3-6
What the Father has done for you

Ephesians 1 shows the Trinity at work on our behalf: "the Father electing (vs. 4-6), the Son redeeming (vs. 7-12) and the Spirit sealing (vs. 13-14), each stanza concluding with the refrain 'to the praise of his glory (vs. 6, 12, 14)." (John Stott) God the Father is the initiator and subject of all the action in this passage. We receive and enjoy his blessing, choosing, predestining, adopting, lavishing us with his grace, all in the "past-tense, done-deal" of these powerful verbs.

b. Who Has Rescued You? — Eph 1:7-12
What Christ has done for you and Who it is all for

Jesus Christ is mentioned 15 times in these first 14 verses of Ephesians. Jesus Christ paid our full debt as slaves to sin with his blood (redemption) so we are now fully forgiven, released from any resentment, any punishment. He chooses not to remember. We are lavished with his grace and love caught up in God's will, purpose and pleasure to unite all things in heaven and earth in Christ. We are part of his purpose and through the unity of the Church display his purposes.

FACT: In Christ. You belong. Even if you don't feel like it. You belong to God the Father, bought with the precious blood of his beloved Son. You are his permanent possession. You are his inheritance and have an inheritance. God also reveals the mystery of his will that all things will be "summed up" in Christ. "Why does God reveal to us this ultimate mystery of the culmination of all things? Because we are central to the plan. The plan to reveal the mystery to us was launched before the foundation of the world was laid (Eph. 1:14, 10); the fulfillment of the plan is at the culmination of the world; and the revelation of both has come to us now. We are at the center of the hourglass of the revealed purpose of God. Why? Because we're part of the plan. . .What this means is that it is now our mission to live out the purpose of God, seeking to unite all things and to submit all to the lordship of Christ." (Bryan Chapell)

c. Who Seals the Deal — Eph 1:13-14
What the Holy Spirit has done for you

The Holy Spirit seals us. In biblical times a seal was a mark of ownership, security, authenticity, and destination. It was branding of belonging, a "protecting sign or a guarantee. . .God seals or stamps them as his own now, and he will protect them through the trials and testings of this life (6:10-18) until he takes final possession of them (vs. 14) on the 'day of redemption' (4:30)." (Peter O'Brien) Guaranteed. God's pledge and promise.

IV. Hear the Refrain — Eph 1:6, 12, 14
To the Praise of His Glory

As Paul highlights what God the Father, God the Son, and God the Holy Spirit have done for believers, he ends each stanza with the refrain that it is all to the praise of his glorious grace (vs. 6) and praise of his glory (vs. 12, 14). "Here then are the 'how' and the 'why' of God's people, who are also his 'heritage' and his 'possession'. *How* did we become his people? Answer: 'According to the good pleasure of his will.' *Why* did he make us his people? Answer: 'For the praise of the glory of his grace.' Thus, everything we have and are in Christ both comes from God and returns to God. It begins in his will and ends in his glory." (John Stott)

V. Hear and Believe the Melody of the Gospel — Eph 1:3-14
Can you hear the melody? Are you singing yet? Are you believing? Pull all the elements together: the individual notes of the Triune God's planning, work on your behalf and pleasure in you; the repeating heartbeat of "in Christ" showing who all these actions take place in; the stanzas showing the Father's election, the Son's redemption and the Spirit's sealing of all believers—Jewish and Gentile. You are no longer your own. We are princes/princesses of purpose, all to the praise of his glory.

Remember Sarah Crewe from *The Little Princess*. "I understand what you're saying but I don't believe it… all girls are princesses…no matter what they look like, where they live, how old they are, where they've been. Their father has told them so." And August Rush, hearing the music of the gospel, knowing he would be rescued and reunited with his family.

This past Friday was one of those days for me where I was living in three very different worlds and praying that each of my dear friends could hear the music of the gospel, hear these truths, walk out their purposes.

Simultaneously Friday night, we celebrated at a wedding of dear friends' son, thinking of their future and all that holds. Other dear friends at probably the same moment were being handed their miracle baby, an adopted son, after years of cancer treatment and infertility, waiting, and other disappointments. Joy in the present moment. Suddenly all the pain and waiting made sense in Christ. Another dear friend was seeing a long line of family and friends at the funeral home, grieving over the death of her dad. She was at peace for him, but full of grief for those left behind. All of these to the praise of his glory. All of these individual puzzle pieces being put together, all being summed up in Christ. Everything in heaven and earth, and all people, Jews and Gentiles coming together as his church.

It's in Christ that we find out who we are and what we are living for. Long before we first heard of Christ and got our hopes up, he had his eye on us, had designs on us for glorious living, part of the overall purpose he is working out in everything and everyone. It's in Christ that you, once you heard the truth and believed it (this Message of your salvation), found yourselves home free—signed, sealed, and delivered by the Holy Spirit. This signet from God is the first installment on what's coming, a reminder that we'll get everything God has planned for us, a praising and glorious life. Ephesians 1:11-14 The Message

In Christ, you are God's adopted son and daughter, fully forgiven and redeemed, his permanent possession, with all the rights, riches, and responsibilities of royalty. You are his prince/princess with a purpose: to be to the praise of his glory.

Week 3: *Living the Unbelievably True Life*
Ephesians 1:15-23

How will you begin experiencing what God has already given you: his hope, riches, and power in Christ?

As we've been studying this first chapter of Ephesians, I've been challenging you to believe it or not. Paul gives you the truth, the head knowledge, but then wisely and effectively prays that it will go from your head to your heart. Doctrine is not enough. God must ignite, illumine, imbed. We always want to know what to "do." Paul gives us the model here: Pray this for yourself and others.

What is prayer? Communication with God. Awareness, acknowledgement of God. St. Teresa of Avila wrote, "Prayer is nothing else than in being on terms of friendship with God." If you've never been in a churched setting, prayer can seem weird, like you are talking to yourself. Remember: You are in two realms. You are located in a physical realm: Birmingham. You're also in a spiritual realm. In many ways, prayer seems simple, but it is the hardest thing to engage in. (Think of all the times you're talking with your friends and then get "down" to praying and the children suddenly erupt in whining, crying, distracting.) Satan hates prayer.

It's already yours. Ask for it. And your glorious, loving Father will give it to you.

I. To know God better — Eph 1:17

Paul knew head knowledge wasn't enough. Any truth that doesn't ignite your heart and activate your hands is empty. What is his solution? Pray. Ephesians 1 is in fact all a prayer.

Verses 3-14 is one long run-on sentence of praise to God for what he has done and given us. He then gives thanks in verses 15-17 and specific petitions in verses 17-19, and closes with praise and lifting up Jesus in verses 20-23. What a great pattern Paul sets.

How do you get truth from your head to your heart? How many of you are struggling because Scripture seems dull? You've heard it all before, you look out and see others getting excited, and you are bored, confused, distracted or skeptical. Or what if you are excited and being changed and you so much want that for someone else? How do you get it into other people's hearts? Paul had been a believer for 20 years. He knew what these Christians struggled with, so he simply and powerfully prays to our glorious Father to make it real to them.

God is the perfect Father. He desires to give it all to us. We will only ask for it as we desperately need it. Paul asks that God give us the spirit of wisdom and revelation. He prays for the Holy Spirit to come so we experience it and apply it. Enlightenment is not an intellectual exercise but a spiritual mystery.

So that you may know him better. Know in Greek is *epignosis*: intimate knowledge. God is a relational God and desires to be in intimate relationship with each of us. He knows us and wants us to know him intimately.

Pray, keep on praying, and ask others to pray that God would make himself, his Word, his promises, his power real to us.

II. To know the hope to which you are called — Eph. 1:18

Eyes of your heart: Heart is the center of emotion. That you would see and be ignited to the core of who you are.

Hope: Future fact. Guaranteed certainty that we move forward in. Not wishful thinking.

Calling: From death to life. Eternal life here and in heaven. Calling is your identity and purpose. "I have called you by name. You are mine."

Riches of his glorious inheritance in the saints. You are a saint. You are his inheritance. You are his joy. His glory. (Zeph 3:17) You are his riches. Individually and corporately. You are sitting in a room of riches.

To know the rich glory of his inheritance in me and every one of his saints is to know my value to him and to be enabled to approach him with great confidence and joy.

Incomparably great power for us who believe. Are you fearful, insecure, out of control? The answer to fear is power. Power: combines two of strongest words possible to describe power *dunamis* dynamite, and *energeia* strength of his might. *Divine dynamic and eternal energy.* Boy do I need that. This power is seen in the resurrection. Brennan Manning calls this resurrection power his *present risenness.* "For me the most radical demand of Christian faith lies in summoning the courage to say yes to the *present risenness* of Jesus Christ."

We see God's love for us and our worth in Christ's death on the cross. We see God's power in raising Jesus to life. It's power present for us NOW.

How are you experiencing the hope of your calling, riches of his glorious inheritance in the saints, incomparable power in Christ? Where are you struggling or in despair? Totally drained and feeling forgotten? Feeling fear and insecurity? Imprisoned? Cry out to God. Ask him to make himself real to you. Give him the specifics. Ask for hope, riches, power. And pray together for these things. Others will believe for you as you believe for them.

III. To know the power you possess through Christ — Eph 1:19-23

Paul finishes this long prayer by turning his eyes to Jesus, glorying over Christ, his position, his power, and his purpose for the Church: We are the called-out ones. The called-together ones. In Ephesians, he gives three pictures of the Church: body, building and bride. It's all about God. It's all about Christ in his fullness. And it's not all about me, it's about the Church.

Jesus is over all. Everything is under him. You are under him. He is your head, your Lord. He fills you with his fullness. He is Lord of this world and the next.

How do you view Christ's power and authority over your life, the Church and the seen and unseen world?

Conclusion:

I always have to ask God to simplify and clarify for me.

If you want it not just in your head, but in your heart, pray.

If you want to know God intimately, pray.

If you want to live a hopeful, rich, powerful life, pray.

If you want it for others and can't force them, pray.

If you want to fulfill your purpose, pray.

That's all we can do. And we can pray together.

We are the Church: the called-out, called-together saints tapping into our promised and available inheritance.

You are God's chosen, lavishly loved adopted son and daughter with all the rights and responsibilities of royalty. You are to the praise of his glory. He longs for you to know and love him as intimately as he knows and loves you. He desires that your heart would awaken to know the hope of your calling, the riches of his glorious inheritance in the saints, in you, and his incomparably great power, which he shows in the resurrection of Jesus Christ. You are forever his. He takes great pleasure in you, not because of anything you do, but just because he is your Abba Father and you are his beloved child. Believe it or not.

Week 4: *Piece of Work or Masterpiece?*
Ephesians 2:1-10

Which of these truths (who you were, what God did for you and why, or who you are called to be now) is the most difficult for you to believe? Why?

The gospel in 10 verses. This is another run-on sentence where Paul pulls past/present/future, all people/Jews/gentiles/mankind, and who we were without Christ, what God has done for us, how and why, and who we now are, where we are, and what our purpose is. Our biggest challenge is to believe it…again and again.

For each of you, you will struggle with a different aspect of the truths of these Scriptures:

Some of you—if you're honest—can't believe you were ever "dead." You still have the illusion you have control over your life, even as you read of that toxic cocktail mixture of the world, Satan, and your flesh influencing you.

Many of you can't believe that God would love you that greatly, that he'd give you this gift, at the cost of his Son—just because he loved you—no strings, no fine print, no hidden requirements.

For others it is hard for you to believe what God isn't calling you a "piece of work." That he has re-created you to be masterpiece (a work of art) to do good works he's already prepared for you.

Pause for a moment and ask yourself where the soap is slipping out of your grasp as you consider God's mercy, love, grace, kindness, and his power and purpose for your life in Christ.

My prayer is that we would all rediscover the wonder of the gospel. Return to being a child and receiving the best possible gift under the Christmas tree, where you clap and laugh and dance and embrace the gift and your Abba Daddy for giving it to you.

I. BUT YOU — Eph 2:1-3
Who You Were

Dead: Really dead. Not like Monty Python's "not dead yet." Dead is dead. Absolute. You're not in the ICU. It's not a situation where you can compare yourself and say you're not as sick as they are. It is not a hospital analogy. It is a graveyard analogy. Kill your illusion of yourself as "pretty good" and competent.

Paul directed this at both gentiles (you) and Jews (we). It is a consolidation of Romans 1-3 in three verses.

Dead: Controlled, enslaved, spiritually unable, zombies, infected. But also walking in it.

Three areas control this "dead man walking:" world, Satan, fleshly desires.

Sins: Missing the mark, any lack of perfection or holiness

Trespasses: Violate a limit, stepping over God's law of love to him or your neighbor. Involves both omission and commission.

Ways of the world: Philips version: "Drifted along the stream of the world's ideas of living."

Ruler of the kingdom of the air/prince of power of air: Satan controls those who are without Christ. Before God's intervention, we are all in this condition.

Disobedient: Doing own thing.

Rebel: Who's in control: Satan, self or God?

By nature, objects/children of wrath: Without Christ, these verses give us a full picture of God, one we don't often want to see. With Christ, we have a new nature, a redeemed relationship with God, sons and daughters with a destiny. Sin separates us from a holy, just and wrathful God.

Wrath is not human anger lashing out in impatience. Wrath is God's holy, contained, sustained fury and hatred of sin and evil. Holiness and wrath go together. You must grasp that fact to wonder at the love of Christ for taking all that justified wrath of God intended for you upon himself on the Cross. Every time you cringe at the word wrath, consider that Jesus took it all for us. The opposite of wrath is not love. It is apathy. "Whatever" (said as a teen with an eye roll) versus passionate love of holiness and hatred of evil.

Our last addiction: Thinking we can or have to save ourselves.

Before Christ: We are prisoners and have drunk the toxic cocktail of the world, Satan, flesh.

We have dear friends, the McLeods, who work with CRU in the Boston area. More than 10 years ago, their then 17-year-old son Zach was in a freak football accident and sustained a horrible brain injury. He survived and has been in a full-time boarding school/rehab facility ever since. He has short-term memory loss, inability to verbally communicate, an unsteady and drawn-up body. He is a prisoner of his body and mind, but his spirit is fully intact. Before the injury, Zach had made a huge impact on his secular Boston prep school because of his kindness, love for his fellow students and his faith. He was set to go onto an Ivy League school and play football. He passionately loved God and had just returned from South Africa where they had a summer ministry to aids orphans and disabled kids. He had prayed with his dad. "What if I were to be like that?" His dad responded, "I'd love you just the same." After the injury, Zach will hobble with help into a waiting room filled with jaded receptionists and other patients and families. His spirit within immediately lights up and connects in love with people. He gives hugs everywhere. If someone mentions prayer, Zach immediately bows his head. He can pray for a long time. He lives constantly in the present moment. His body is broken, his brain injured but his soul is alive!

II. BUT GOD — Eph 2:4-7
What God Did and Why

Verses1-3 bring us to the end of ourselves. There is nothing we can do.

But then we have the gospel condensed in two words: **But God.**

Can God be both wrathful and loving? Read verses 4-5.

Because of his great love for us, because of his rich mercy, because of his grace and kindness, God. There's the mystery and vastness of God: A God who is loving and holy, just and merciful, wrathful and gracious. How does he stay consistent to himself? Through the Cross. His love provides for our salvation, our redemption through the blood of his son, Jesus Christ. We are loved "in Christ." Immeasurable, inconceivable, surpassing. In Ephesians 1:20, Paul describes God's power in raising Jesus from the dead. In Ephesians 2:7 he describes God's love as shown through Cross of Jesus Christ.

Look at the heaping, stacking, layer on layer of descriptions: rich in mercy, great love which he loved us, grace, gift, kindness. Can you believe it? Watchman Nee, Chinese believer and minister imprisoned for his faith, wrote this,

"God is so very, very rich. It gives him true joy when we just let him give and give and give again to us. It is a grief to him, too, when we try to do things for him, for he is so very, very able. He longs that we just let him do and do and do. For he wants to be the giver eternally, and he wants to be the doer eternally. If only we saw how rich and how great God is, we would leave all the giving and all the doing to him."

The grace of God is love freely shown toward guilty sinners, contrary to their merit and in defiance of their demerit. It is God showing goodness to persons who deserve only severity and had no reason to expect anything but severity.

Grace: Getting what I don't deserve

Mercy: Not getting what I do deserve

Seated with Christ in the heavenly realms: Note it is past tense. How would that change your view of life if you understood being seated with Christ?

Seated: Finished. Resting. Trusting. Secure. We must be seated before setting out for Christ.

Our purpose: To reflect individually and corporately to the angels God's character (his grace, kindness, wisdom).

But we have to get a handle on what we were by nature. Our inability to save ourselves and God's total ability and initiation. But God. Only God.

Visual Aid

Write this out on board and edit it down:

Truth: God loves me in spite of my sin.

What do I emphasize? God loves me **in spite** of my sin.

Can I edit it? God loves me in ~~spite of~~ my sin.

Truth: God loves me in my sin.

But can I edit it even further?

God loves me ~~in my sin~~.

God loves me. God loves me. Period.

Do you hear the "but, but, buts?"

Lie Guy: How could he love you in spite of all your sins? Why?

Truth Teller: Just because.

Are you beginning to rediscover the wonder of it all?

III. BUT NOW, BY GRACE — Eph 2:8-10
Who You Are Now

Begin putting the puzzle pieces together. Who you are now and who you are called to be and to know it as an adventure from beginning to end. God loves you. God has saved you (perfect tense. It is past and present and future tense all in one!)

For by grace, you have been saved. Not of yourself. Not of works. A gift of God, so no one can boast.

How do you receive gifts? With suspicion, guilt, pure delight, already figuring out what you have to give back?

How can you explain both the humility and wonder of grace? They go together. We want something to do with it, so we'll get a little credit. It's like asking your husband. Why do you love me? He'd better have a good answer, even if it's "just because. . ."

Tale of Three Vacations:

My spiritual gift is vacationing. I receive it well. I share it well. I even virtual vacation well. My husband does not share that gift. Here's a few of our vacationing moments so you can understand what grace feels like and what it doesn't:

Vacation #1: Hilton Head. Really poor in the middle of medical school. Someone offered for us to use their little house at Hilton Head because they were going to be gone for the weekend. I was so excited. We got there. Saturday was great. We rode bikes. Soaked up sun on the beach. Sunday, we spent the whole day cleaning their house, rooms we hadn't even been in because Bill felt so guilty. They called us up that night and wanted to know if we wanted to come every month!

Vacation #2: We got to go to Vail with good friends who were friends with a megawealthy woman who just wanted to bless them. She paid for all of us to stay in this slopeside condo with everything. I relished it. Lifestyle of the rich and famous. Bill not so much. The last night, he asked her if he could help pay for it. She shrugged and said if he wanted to. We left really early the next day. As he looked at the invoice, he made me call Visa to see if we could cover it. That was a very long drive to Denver. We now can laugh and call those "Vail units," like that new mountain bike would be like only two Vail units.

Vacation #3: For our 30th wedding anniversary, we splurged and signed up for a bed and breakfast for one night at the Henderson Park Inn at Destin. Then a friend "gave us" his huge house for a week at Sea Grove because a renter cancelled at the last minute. At the Henderson Park Inn, I (the grinch of the universe) calculated everything to see if it was worth what we paid. The air conditioning vent was broken. We didn't get our chocolate on our pillow. Because we paid, I had really high expectations. We had "earned" the best.

But at this beach home, it was all grace. From the moment we walked into the house, I started calling folks to see if they wanted to come and share it with us. Too good to be true. It was very humbling to receive when we didn't deserve it. Bill kept saying but we should, but by then, I'd found my voice and reminded him of the Vail units. And told him to learn to just be grateful and humble and receive.

By grace through faith. It is a gift of God, not of yourselves (you were dead, remember?) So that no one would boast or take some credit.

By grace: Another great two-word definition of the gospel. Nothing in me deserves this. I receive it through faith. Resting, surrendering, placing trust in Jesus.

Let go of "doing" and grab hold of "it is done."

Penelope Stokes, "True faith is not a matter of personal strength, not an issue of quantity, not a question of how much certainty we can muster to meet our needs. Biblical faith, rather, is a dependence upon the person in whom we claim to believe. True faith focuses not upon the believer's ability to believe, but upon the grace and faithfulness of God."

The big question is not how much faith do you have, but who is the object of your faith?

Who you gonna' believe? Yourself (you're dead), the world, Satan, or the God who has great love and mercy and grace and kindness for you?

Who are you now?

Workmanship: Work of art, poem, masterpiece, not a piece of work. Created in Christ Jesus to do good works, God's work, prepared in advance for you to do. There is a mention of works but in the right order: Unable. But God, made alive, raised, seated.

You must first be seated with Christ before setting out for Christ. You will display God's glory, just by being you. If God has the power to make you alive, he has the power to fulfill his purpose through you. You are a prince/princess with a purpose. God's purpose.

Remember who you were, what he has done and what he has promised to make you and rest in that. When you read verse 10, you can either fear that you will blow it or you can see it in light of the already true truths, already prepared and enabled works.

Conclusion

Remember in Christ you are a lavishly loved, chosen, adopted son and daughter of the King with all the privileges and responsibilities of royalty.

Remember without Christ you were dead, controlled by your flesh, the world, Satan and were objects of wrath.

Remember two sets of gospel definitions: But God. By grace.

Remember what God did for you and why he did it and what he has planned for you and rest in it. Only God is able to save you. Only God is able to fulfill you. He has already done it.

Which of these truths are hardest for you to believe?

Who you were

What God has done for you and that he loves you. Period. Just because.

What God has called and empowered you to be and do.

Let's pray:

O God: Restore to us the joy of our salvation, renew our wonder and awe at what you have done for us and what you have planned for us. We thank you, Jesus, for taking our wrath upon yourself on the Cross. We worship you, God, in your holiness, love, mercy, grace and kindness. God, if there are any who are struggling to know whose they are, I pray that through faith, they would look to Jesus. May we be as little children delighting in the opening of a gift beyond our highest hopes and fondest dreams.

Week 5: *God's Great Mystery Revealed*
Ephesians 2:11 – 3:13

In the midst of hostility, brokenness, insecurity and loneliness, Jesus Christ is our peace and our cornerstone and our access to God.

As God reveals that his wisdom and glory will be displayed in Christ and through his church, how will it change your view of and participation in the church?

First, let's review where Paul has taken us in Ephesians:

Theme: Peace through grace.

Truth: In Christ

Purpose: *To bring all things in heaven and earth together under one head, Christ.* (Eph 1:10)

In these verses Paul unveils the mystery how God will reveal himself to the world and the heavenly realms

Method: In Christ, through his church (of Jews and Gentiles together)

I. The Gospel According to John...Lennon
Peace and Access in Christ — Ephesians 2:11-22

John Lennon's song "Imagine" is his response to Christianity. But imagine his frustration, his own longing. Seeing the world through his own reality. There is a disputed letter he wrote to Oral Roberts wondering about Christianity and revealing his own painful background. What if he could imagine his life and the world through the invitation of Scripture?

https://www.youtube.com/watch?v=bb3EgckGnOA

As you read the rest of Ephesians 2, remember it is anchored in who you were, what God did, who you are now. We now read the reality of your preordained "work" in light of the reality of the world. It's a place of aliens, filled with loneliness, insecurity, hostility, no peace. Paul reveals the three threads of book: Peace through grace. In Christ. Through Church.

Ephesians 2:11-3:13 are crucial verses to understand individually, and even more importantly, corporately as the Church. (Not as your individual denomination or church building, but the universal Church filled with saints, the Bride of Christ, the Body of believers.)

American culture meets true Christianity. I was raised a good American. If you try hard enough, you'll make it, on your own. Independence is a core American value. Do not rely on anyone else. When I became a Christian, I just adapted it, not to biblical Christianity but Nancy's American Christianity. Instead of it all depending on me, now it was me and God. I thought I was getting really holy when I changed the order to "God and me." Honestly, I would still prefer that. So much easier, less messy, less painful, and so much more under my control. Biblical Christianity says we are one in Christ, and it is through the oneness of the Church that God will be glorified and revealed. The oneness of redeemed and broken sinners.

What about you? Would Christianity be more appealing if God would just take away all those other messy people and the call to work it out together?

A. Jesus Christ is Our Peace—Ephesians 2:11-18

What we have dealt with individually in Ephesians 2:1-10, we deal with corporately in these verses.

Gentiles: All non-Jews were considered "dogs." They were without Christ, without hope. As you read that and look out on your family, your neighborhood, your workplace, the divisions in the world, how does that grip you? But now in Christ, they are brought near. What God has planned for us together will shock and amaze the angels and the heavenly realms and the world around us.

Christ Jesus is our peace. He is our shalom, our wholeness. In him, all things make sense. The Bible is a book of redemption, reconciliation, restoration and renewed relationships, man to God, man to self, and man to man.

Peace through grace: Remember definition of grace. All God's doing: in Jesus Christ.

Cross: It reaches vertically (God to man) and horizontally (man to man).

Dividing wall between Gentiles and Jews. Best analogy for our culture is racial injustice. In the time of Ephesians, they had to tear down not only the dividing wall of hostility but the way they had been built. Archeologists found a sign at one of these walls that said, "Anyone arrested there will have himself to blame for the penalty of death that will be imposed as a consequence."

Our best friends were missionaries in Israel for 20 years. What a living picture of the hostility and the only hope: Jesus Christ is our peace. Our friend, Paul, was harassed by Jews and Palestinians alike and his basic message was only through Yeshua is our shalom. They developed a children's ministry where both Jewish and Palestinian believers participated. It's one of the few displays of hope in this divided country. Know Jesus, know peace. No Jesus, no peace.

Where do you have walls of hostility? Peace is not absence of conflict but a unity only possible through Jesus. Where are you not one with someone? Husband, child, in-laws, parents, siblings, family, friends, work associates, church members, political divides, denominations? You know the difference between truce and peace. Bring it to Jesus. Through the Cross, through his blood, be at peace. These walls often have so much to do with rights and being right. The Jews were relying on the external appearance of the law. The Gentiles saw through their self-righteousness. Today, we see the same walls and reactions to the "upright" people and all those outside of that. Are you willing to allow the Cross to bring you all to the same place of total dependence on Christ? It means letting go of rights, letting go of grievances, history, even your American values.

B. Jesus Christ is Our Cornerstone—Ephesians 2:19-22

Paul paints a visual of the church: family, building, holy temple. The Gentiles knew what it felt like to be aliens and strangers. So did the Jews, through their multiple captivities. To be a citizen carries great weight. Paul goes on to tell the Gentiles they are now members of God's household, part of the family. In the best of families, there is a feeling of security and safety.

Paul uses the building analogy for the Church with the foundation, the cornerstone, and the building blocks. The *foundation* of the apostles and prophets refers to the New Testament anointed teachers of the church. The *cornerstone* helps to hold the building steady and keeps it in line. The emphasis was not on a physical temple (which was destroyed in 70 AD), but on a spiritual, international community. John Stott writes, "This is where God dwells. He is not tied to a holy building but to holy people, to his own new society. To them he has pledged himself by a solemn covenant. He lives in them, individually and as a community."

II. Masterpiece Theatre Presents: Mystery!
His Church Reveals His Wisdom Ephesians 3:1-13

A. Paul's Call Ephesians 3:1-13

Paul believes in God's sovereignty, calling himself a prisoner for (or *of*) Christ Jesus. Even though he was technically a prisoner of Nero, this too was under God's control.

Paul then speaks in amazement and true humility about his calling from God, calling himself the "leastest of the leastest," (3:8) even possibly playing off his name Paul which means little. "'I am little,' he may be saying, 'little by name, little in stature, and morally and spiritually littler than the littlest of the Christians.' He is deeply conscious both of his own unworthiness . . . and of Christ's overflowing mercy towards him . . . his modesty . . . did not hinder him from taking responsibility as an apostle . . . he combined personal humility with apostolic authority. Indeed, while 'minimizing himself he magnified his office.'" (John Stott)

Spiritual maturity is not getting better and better but getting a better and better view of yourself and God. Which will leave you humble and amazed and glorifying God that He loves you and can use you.

The privilege and compelling of God's call to preach the mystery of the gospel to the gentiles stayed with Paul all his life, even to suffering (3:13) and dying for the gospel to reach the gentiles.

What about you? Where do you feel small? Least? Imprisoned? A misfit? Right where you are at, in your prison, God has called you, given you a unique privilege, to use his resources to reconcile, to make peace, to present the unsearchable riches of Christ.

B. Mystery #1: No Way! Them, Too?—Ephesians 3:1-6

When a good mystery novel or play reveals the ending, there is a sense of satisfaction that all the pieces of the puzzle are now in place, that it all now makes sense. It ties back into the theme of Ephesians in verse 1:10 where all things in Heaven and Earth will be summed up (or make sense) in Christ. The "solved" mystery involves the people of God becoming the church of God in Christ.

The first part of the mystery is the double union of Jews and Gentiles with Christ and each other. Because of the centuries of separation and hostility, this revelation would have been a shock to the Jews, especially that Gentiles were now sharing equally the same inheritance with the Jews. Jews considered them a subcategory of humanity. They had to change their whole way of thinking.

Do not take this full reconciliation of all races and peoples lightly. Most American churches have yet to experience the richness of true new-humanity worship of all races, tongues, and people groups. Often, we're still too concerned about denominational differences, racial boundaries and political issues.

C. Mystery #2: Multi-Colored Wisdom—Ephesians 3:7-13

This second part of the mystery is that through the church, God's manifold (or multicolored, multifaceted) wisdom will be displayed to the heavenly authorities (with the focus being on angels). The angels can't conceive of grace and mercy (never having sinned). It is as we, redeemed sinners, love one another, that we show the grace and mercy of God to the sinless angels.

This gospel of the riches of Christ that "Paul preached is that he died and rose again not only to save sinners like me (though he did), but also to create a single new humanity; not only to redeem us from sin but also to adopt us into God's family; not only to reconcile us to God but also to reconcile us to one another . . . The gospel is good news of a new society as well as of a new life." (John Stott)

So often, especially as Americans, we don't even realize the pervasiveness of the independent values we have been raised with. We think it holy to switch it from "Just Me and God" to "God and Me." Adding too many people, especially people unlike ourselves, it becomes messy and out of our control.

God's "open secret" is that through His Church he will be glorified. "Our witness should not simply be about 'Jesus and me,' or about gaining approval, or even about my living for the glory of God; it is about seeing the glory of bringing many people together of different and distasteful and even antagonistic backgrounds and having them together come freely and confidently before the Father to glory in the grace of the Savior. By loving the unlovely, showing grace to the angry, being forgiving toward the hurtful, and being bold without bitterness in the face of attack, we show the glory of the wisdom of God to men and angels." (Bryan Chapell)

Living to God's eternal purpose in Christ will lead to a bold, confident, free life where we take advantage of full access to the God the Father through his Spirit (vs. 12). But Paul realizes how unbelievably true these verses are, so he will once again pray to the Father that we will know and experience the love of Christ and power of God in the next part of his letter, Ephesians 3:14-21.

You have the privilege because of Christ of approaching your Abba Father and King in freedom and confidence.

Let's pray:

God, thank you for Jesus Christ, our peace, our cornerstone. Thank you for the reality of who we are individually and together in Christ. Thank you for the hope of restored relationships with our family, friends, church and others. We ask that you make us a true body of believers able to work together and love one another, knowing that brings you glory, knowing that this amazes the angels. Let us be bold and beloved children as we come confidently and freely to our Father's throne. Give us the peace of Christ in our churches.

Week 6: *Living the "So Much More" Life*
Ephesians 3:14-21

Where do you need to experience the Spirit's power, Christ's love, God's fullness in the mystery of your life? Where are you waiting and wondering if God is able to do more for you and through you?

I just ate at Full Moon BBQ and I was so tempted to get their t-shirt "Best Butts in Town."

Ephesians has some of the best "buts" (single t) in Scripture:

Chapter 1: "But in Christ" spiritual blessings of who we are. In Christ all will make sense.

Chapter 2: "But you" were dead in your sins. "But God" by the riches of his mercy and "by grace," you are saved. "But now" we are brought near by the blood of Christ.

Chapter 3: But not alone! The mystery is that together Jews and gentiles as his church bring God glory.

Paul calls the Ephesians to be bold and go to their Abba's throne. He also says to "not lose heart, my suffering is for your glory."

If we keep with the prince/princess analogy, we've gone from seeing ourselves as sons/daughters of the king to princes/princesses not paupers, to princes/princesses not prisoners, to princes/princesses with purpose and power, to a pile of princes/princesses together. And now, I think Paul is addressing "perplexed" princes/princesses

We've gone from "but you" to "but God" to by grace and "but now" to "but wait!" If I am a prince/princess, don't I get to now live happily ever after? Look at verse 13. "So I ask you not to lose heart over what I am suffering for you, which is for your glory."

The reality is that Paul is in prison suffering. The reality is that the Ephesian believers are people in pain. The Ephesian Jews who have come to faith have been ostracized by their families for following this new cult. Many of the Ephesian gentiles have come out of dark places (sorcery, idolatry, temple prostitution) and are disdained by the Jews who have been raised to consider them dogs.

These new Christians are trying to hear and believe all Paul is saying about them, even as they look around. Remember the scene from The Little Princess? Mrs. Minchen mocking and screaming, "Do you still fancy yourself a princess? Look around you. Why just look in the mirror." Sara Crewe responds, "I am a princess. All girls are. Even if you live in an attic, even if you wear rags, even if you're not pretty or smart or young. We are all princesses. Didn't your father ever tell you that? Didn't he?"

Paul desires for us as believers to go from being perplexed, struggling with the "I tried, and I haven't gotten what I asked or imagined" to powerful princes and princesses with perspective, deeply loved sons and daughters, even if we find ourselves still in an attic waiting for an answer.

How are you experiencing these verses?

Thinking about tornadoes in Alabama. Your house spared while those around you destroyed? Or yours destroyed while others untouched? Did one person pray harder than the other? Is life random or does that prayer only work for others, not you?

Where do you struggle with these verses? Where is it hard to experience Christ's love for you?

My default is often I'm glad he loves you and can see it, but I don't think he loves me. How could he? Can you honestly trust that God is working mightily and more than you can imagine on your behalf?

I. For This Reason — Eph 3:14-15
Paul's Pivotal Prayer

For this reason links back to 3:1, and also chapters 1-3. Paul is preparing them to live and experience Christ's love for them and walk out chapters 4-6. We are coming to his pivotal hinge prayer linking *who we are* with *how we live it out.*

We must be rooted and grounded in love. Paul realizes if we don't believe we are loved infinitely beyond our head knowledge, we will not be able to live out who we are called to be in chapters 4-6. We will burn out or become bitter or back away.

The love that motivates us is actually the power that drives us. In Ephesians 3:14-21, Paul wants us to know that "when we grasp the love of Christ, we are filled with the power of God. . . love for Christ drives out love for the things of the world. and our love for Christ must first spring from an awareness of his love for us." (Bryan Chapell)

Paul realizes that they need to know experientially what they have been processing intellectually. They must have courage to trust, that in the midst of their current lives, the Spirit's power in them, Christ's love for them, and God's filling of them is their ultimate reality.

Ephesians is a book of different progressing positions or postures: Dead. Sit. Kneel. Walk. Stand.

In Ephesians 3, Paul kneels, when it was customary to stand. It was a sign of deep reverence for God, humility of being part of his family, and passion for his people.

Eph 1 prayer: Focus is on enlightenment (to see/believe it).

Eph 3 prayer: Focus is on empowerment (to live it out) and enthronement (for Christ to dwell in your heart by faith).

II. Are You "Feeling" It? — Eph 3:16-19
A Prayer to Experience the Triune God's Power, Love and Fullness

Paul's prayers are bigger, bolder, and more courageous than I would dare to pray on my own. John Stott sees this prayer as a "staircase by which he climbs higher and higher in his aspiration for his readers. His prayer-staircase has four steps, whose key words are 'strength', 'love', 'knowledge' and 'fullness.'"

The first step: **Power.**

Paul prays we will experience divine spirit-strength for divine Christ-indwelling. when Paul talks about *Christ dwelling in our hearts*, it means to settle down permanently, not to stay for a few nights.

The second step: **Love.**

Paul mixes agrarian (rooted) and architectural (established, built up) metaphors to stress that "love is the soil in which believers are rooted and will grow, the foundation upon which they are built." (Peter O'Brien)

The third step ties infinite love to incomprehensible **knowledge.**

It is so inconceivable that this step must be taken in community with other believers. We can't know the love of Christ in isolation. "It needs the whole people of God to understand the whole love of God, all the saints together, Jews and gentiles, men and women, young and old, black and white, with all their varied backgrounds and experiences." (John Stott)

Paul gives infinite, expanding dimensions to Christ's love: "A love that is wide enough to embrace the world (John 3:16); a love that is long enough to last forever (1 Cor. 13:8); a love that is high enough to take sinners to heaven (1 John 3:1, 2); and a love which is deep enough to take Christ to the very depths to reach the lowest sinner (Phil. 2:8)."(Kent Hughes)

The fourth step: **fullness.**

This fullness (which is in passive voice meaning God is the one doing the filling) refers to God's presence, life and power. Paul is praying that these believers would open up their lives to be filled with God's fullness so they will be spiritually mature.

No better illustration of the love of Christ than the Cross, I love the story of Napoleon's men finding a skeleton in dungeon with a cross on wall with labels: height, depth, length, breadth.

Length: as long as eternity

Breadth: people from every tribe and nation

Height: as high as heaven. His love carries us home to heaven.

Depth: as deep as hell. No matter how deep a hell you are, Christ's love is deeper.

But do you love me?
Brennan Manning tells how he took the name of his best boyhood friend, Brennan, who in battle threw himself on a grenade to save Brennan Manning and the rest of the men. Brennan became a priest author and speaker. After a successful speaking engagement, he was attacked with doubts. Did God really love him? He went back to his friend's mother, a simple Irish woman caring for a mentally disabled adult son. As Brennan sat with her, in simple silence, he finally broke down and asked, did your son, Brennan, love me? It was the first time he ever saw the gentle lady get angry as she cried out, "What more could he ha'done for ya?"

As you struggle with doubt, consider again and again the breadth and length and height and depth of Christ's love for you personally in the Cross.

Let yourself experience it. Love hurts.

Practical ways to dwell on Christ's love, god's fullness:

Be in Scripture. Be in community (with all the saints). Pray Scripture. Meditate on Christ's actions on your behalf: his incarnation, his life, his death on the Cross, his resurrection, his intercession.

III. The "So Much More" Life — Eph 3:20-21
Do you want God to do more than you ask or do exactly what you ask and no more?

He is superabundantly able and willing to do more than you ask or think or even imagine. I realized I don't always want that. I want exactly what I ask for when I ask for it. I want what I imagine, what I think I want (all to the glory of God if it doesn't get in my way of course!).

What if God wants more for each of us? A "more" we cannot even conceive on this side of Heaven? "Our requests are feeble and finite. We want dessert when we need meat, success when we need humility, and safety when we need godly courage—or Christlike sacrifice. We ask within the limits of human vision, but he is able to do more. He sees into eternity what is needful for our soul and for the souls of those whom our lives will touch across geography and across generations; and seeing this, he is able to do more than we ask." (Bryan Chapell)

This prayer has been my prayer so often and God has answered in a "more than I asked for" way.

Infertility: As we went through multiple treatments and multiple disappointments, I felt like a failure. I felt foolish. That God laughed at my prayers. From this side, with our adopted children, I can look back and realize the "so much more" answer! Even as I still deal with the unfulfilled longings on wanting to bear children on my own.

Many of us have walked with in deep, long places where we have boldly gone to the throne and our prayers seems to be shelved. Or we received things we not wanted.

Paul says: Be bold! Trust your father! Remember the mystery that in Christ and in the church, he will be glorified. Remember we are his masterpieces. We still are putting together the puzzle with no picture on the front of the box. It is all coming together but we can't quite see it. It is scary to have the God of the universe who deeply loves me answer my heart's prayers.

Truth Teller: Christ loves me more than I can know. God is at work in my life more than I can imagine.

Let's pray: O perfect Father, full of glorious riches, we confess that we don't always believe how much you love us, how much Jesus loves us. We confess that we don't feel your power in our lives. But most of all, we confess that we want your power to fix our problems, we want your power to get to an easier place. We think you don't love us if we are in pain. Forgive us for often feeling like abandoned, orphaned princes/princesses. What more could you have done? You have told us and demonstrated your love for us on the Cross, your power in the resurrection. What more could you do than to put us in this greatest adventure for your Kingdom? Help us to trust you and believe you. Make us trusting, powerful princes/princesses and give us perspective in the midst of our longings and confusions. We can't conceive of your love, Jesus. We can't imagine what you're doing in our lives. Help us to believe it and pray for full lives, full of the fullness of God.

Week 7: *Time to Grow Up*
Ephesians 4:1-16

How will you start spending your inheritance? How will you strive for unity, use your unique gifts, and grow up together in love?

As we begin Ephesians 4, we transition from doctrine to duty, from understanding our inheritance to investing in it, from being seated with Christ to setting out in Christ. You are ready for the privileges and response-ability of royalty.

Begin with a movie clip from *The Princess Diaries*.

https://www.youtube.com/watch?v=bZvMSQGigGI

Showing scene where Mia reads the letter her prince father left for her on her 16th birthday as she's about to run away, abdicate her throne out of fear of failure. "Courage not the absence of fear, but the judgment that there's something more important than that fear. From who you think you are to who you can be (or in a biblical sense…who you really are), the key is to make the journey." This scene shows that Mia "gets" what it means to walk worthy of your calling. not about "I and me" but we—and what we—with all our different giftings can do together for the Kingdom, for the church. What does it mean to walk out your calling?

I. Live It Up! — Eph 4:1-6
Walk out who you are together

Do you really believe who you are in Christ? His masterpiece. His beloved son and daughter. Do you believe what you've been called and enabled to do? That's the key. Paul prays that we'd be empowered and be rooted in love and trust the God who is able to do so much more than we can ask or imagine.

Walk worthy. Live the life. Embrace your calling: in Christ, seated with him, works prepared for you, use your inheritance.

Humble/lowly: Accurate picture of yourself—not too highly, not too lowly. A life of double knowledge: knowing God, knowing self.

Gentleness/meekness: "That temper of soul in which we accept his dealings with us as good, and therefore without disputing or resisting." (Vines) It is not weakness, but strength under submission, like a racehorse allowing bit in his mouth.

Patience/longsuffering: That "quality of self-restraint in the face of provocation which does not hastily retaliate or promptly punish. It is the opposite of anger and is associated with mercy and is used of God…patience is the quality that does not surrender to circumstances or succumb under trial; it is the opposite of despondency and is associated with hope." (Vines)

Bearing with one another in love: Paul has prayed that we would be rooted and grounded in love through the power of the Holy Spirit, which is the only way to keep on bearing with one another in agape (self-sacrificial, godly) love. Striving, every effort, for unity in the Spirit.

This is the "so much more life." So much more humility, gentleness, patience, love to give others than I imagined. It's counterintuitive. My intuition says I've "loved" enough, graced enough. It's time to grab my rights. What if it's so much more than you imagined? More than you can do on own. My "love" quota is so low, especially for my own family. Experiment with counterintuitive grace and love.

Unity: Paul gives a seven-fold list broken into three parts representing the Trinity:

One body (church). One Spirit.

One hope (Jesus Christ, his resurrection, his calling of you, his purpose and plan). One Lord (Jesus Christ). One faith. One baptism (not speaking of mode of baptism, but identification with Jesus Christ. An outward sign of inward reality like circumcision).

One God and Father of all in all.

The first identifying mark of church: Unity in love.

Where will you live the so much more life of counterintuitive, more-than-you-thought, more-than-you-can-do love?

II. Build Up! — Eph 4:7-13

Use your Christ-given unique gifts for the church

Here, when speaking of grace, it refers not to saving grace but serving grace. Grace as the gift given to you for building up and serving the church.

Paul goes from unity to diversity. All parts are unique, but they fit together. Unity is not uniformity. Think of the puzzle pieces being put together. All different colors and shapes and sizes, but as they are put together, they show a beautiful picture of Christ. It is a picture of all different parts of a body growing together into the head.

This is where we often feel like the stepsister. We don't know or we doubt the value of our own gift. We long for someone else's gift, to do something else (maybe more important or prominent) for the kingdom.

"Happiest are those who discover Christ's gift and give themselves to excel in what God has made them to do—whether that is preaching or teaching or evangelizing or writing or making music or making money or giving counsel or showing hospitality or creating art—according to the gift that the Lord God has given. . . .the Christians that I know who have made the greatest shipwreck of their lives (for reasons other than blatant sin) are those who have not been satisfied with fulfilling the calling of their specific gifts. They always wanted to be someone else. . . love what God has made you to be and believe he is using you even in difficult places. Such confidence that he is giving himself to the church through you will be the source of the deepest satisfaction of your life." (Bryan Chapell)

Do you know how Christ has gifted you to build up the body? Are you excited about your gifting? Are you being equipped or equipping others? What has God given you a passion for, what makes you excited or come alive?

There's a great children's book called *Cinderedna*. It winsomely shows the truth we're all unique. Live out who you are and in so doing build up those around you.

What is your gifting or calling? How will you find out? How will you use it for church?

III. Grow Up! — Eph 4:14-16
Grow up together in love in Christ.

These opening verses in chapter 4 speak of Paul's vision for the church to display charity, unity, diversity, and maturity. We're not to be like Peter Pan ("I won't grow up!") Like Princess Mia, we've got to make a decision to make the journey and make it together. We decide to grow up. to no longer be babies.

We live in dangerous times where we allow ourselves to be tossed by different media and politics often with a religious label. When we are to dig deep into Scriptural truth (the giftings above –apostle, prophet, evangelist, pastor, teacher—all deal with sound teaching) and not be swayed by the next formula, technique, opinion. Weigh all things. Be in solid community for help in discerning. Be in prayer. Be in Scripture.

Build up. Speak truth in love. "In love" is the 'inclusion' the bookends, the heartbeat of the church. we show unity in love in Christ.

Speak truth in love: "Truthing" in love—words, actions, walk. Always ask, what's your motivation in speaking "truth?"

End with another movie clip. *Mr. Holland's Opus.*

https://www.youtube.com/watch?v=tQqjIVUQdTI

Mr. Holland is a music teacher from a public high school, always dreamed of being a composer but was supporting his wife and deaf son and faithfully pouring into generations of students' lives. In this scene, he's old, the music program has been cut and he has cleaned out his desk. He feels like he's been a failure. As you watch this and listen, ask yourself what part do you play? What lives do you touch?

Together we are Christ's great symphony. We all play different instruments together as Christ's magnus opus. God's mysterious masterpiece together.

You are essential, needed. You may not be rich or famous. But look around you. You are the music of someone's life, just as they in different way are your music. Just as Princess Mia heard from her father: the key is to make the journey. To keep on walking.

Let's pray

God our Father, please help us remember and believe what you have called us to be, who we are in Christ, what we have. That we are loved daughters and sons of the king, seated in the heavenlies in Christ. We are beloved, royal children. But it is so hard. Our experience tells us differently. Help us to believe you, our true reality! Help us to live it out in love with one another. That we would grow in unity, that each one would know our calling and how wev are uniquely gifted and needed. I pray for each person here to grow up together, to be willing to be in community, to speak the truth in love, to build each other up. And that you, O God, would receive all the glory! As we are your your magnus opus, your masterpiece, together.

Week 8: *The Cinderella Syndrome*
Ephesians 4:17-5:21

Where do you need to waltz in your new clothes? How will you begin living loved and "holy ever after" this week?

Think of that deeply theological woman, Cinderella. She's in the ash heap, scrubbing up after her wicked stepsisters. Poof! Suddenly her fairy godmother waves her magic wand and she's transformed into a beautiful princess with the perfect gown and glass slippers. She's swept off her feet by Prince Charming. Then reverse poof! She knew it was too good to be true. She's back in the ashes, in her rags, serving her stepsisters and stepmother, who are only too glad to see her back in her place. But all the time, the prince is pursuing her. He finds her, clothes her in a beautiful gown, marries her, and they live happily ever after. Really? Don't you want to know the rest of the story? Do you think she worried about keeping the prince pleased? Her new gown clean? The castle spic and span? How she'd deal with the stepsisters accusing her of being an imposter? How would she live like who she really was?

Like Cinderella, we have been in the ash heap, helpless. *But God. By grace.* We have been transformed and are alive with Christ, our prince, and seated with him on his throne. But now, we get to live as his royalty, his masterpieces, in this "now-not-yet" kingdom. But it is not a fairy tale. It is a battleground, and our first battle is to believe, believe who we really are now in Christ. Read these "calls to action" in Ephesians 4-5 not from a place of fear (what if he finds out I'm really just Cinderella, and not really a beautiful princess? that I'm still failing, still sinning) but from the rooted place of love (walking in love as a dearly loved son and daughter). read Eph. 4:17-24, Col. 1:10-14

I. Once Upon a Time — Eph 4:17-24
Once upon a time. When you hear those words, you settle in for a fairy tale, a great adventure which will end with the words "they lived happily ever after." Today, I want you to settle in for a great story, but as a Christian, it's all real and it's your story. an unbelievably true story of rescue and redemption from the domain of darkness to the kingdom of light, the kingdom of his Son. You do live in an enchanted kingdom, where your biggest battle, if you are a believer, is to believe who you really are, because it's so unbelievably true. In this story there is no fairy godmother with a magic wand. we have our Triune God.

Look at Eph. 4:30-5:2. The loving, forgiving, heavenly Father and king (Eph 4:32-5:1). The rescuing, redeeming, sacrificing prince and king, Jesus Christ (Eph 5:2). The assuring, sealing, grieving, sanctifying, and very real Holy Spirit (Eph 4:30) who acts like the fairy godmother in "magically," supernaturally transforming us to become who we really are.

If we're living out this great Christian adventure, how do we go from *once upon a time* to happily—or as a believer what God calls and accomplishes for us—*holy ever after?* How do we live out our new lives together in this now-not-yet kingdom as we await the return of our king?

I call it the *Cinderella Syndrome*. Your biggest fear is that this transformation is too good to be true and the clock will strike midnight and, poof! you'll go back to the real you, back to your rags. That as you sit on the throne with this pursuing prince in the new realm (Eph 2), all those old stepsisters who knew who you were are still out there laughing at you. And you keep looking in the mirror wiping away the cinders from your face, looking down on your beautiful gown, wondering if you scrubbed the floors, the prince would keep loving you. You battle feelings that you are a fake and will fail. Are you really who they say you are? Inside it doesn't feel like it. If they really knew me! Your biggest battle is to believe who you really are.

a. The Old Kingdom: Once We Walked Alone — Eph 4:17-19

Paul calls them to remember who they were and to no longer walk like that (Eph 4:17). Walking is all through Ephesians. it is *peripatevw* in Greek. What a great ordinary word for the extraordinary adventure of living out of this new life. it's how you daily step, behave, conduct your life. You were the walking dead (Eph 2:2). Now, as adopted sons and daughters, redeemed by the blood of his son Jesus, walk in a manner worthy of your calling (4:1). Don't walk like the gentiles (4:17). Walk in love (5:2). Walk in light (5:8). Walk wisely (5:15). Listen to your Abba: Believer, do not fear. I am with you. I am walking hand in hand with you. I will accomplish it for you. But walk with me. Trust me, step by step.

The Ephesian believers, primarily gentiles, are surrounded by the pagan culture around them, the magic city, filled with family and friends still living the alienated life. Look at this description, so like the Romans 1 "death spiral," Col. 1:13's domain of darkness, Eph. 2's walking dead. They walk in the futility of their minds, darkened in their understanding. Futility is dark and empty purposelessness. They are alienated, estranged, walking alone and separated from God on a vertical plane and horizontally from others.

Why? Because of their hardened hearts. Moral arteriosclerosis of the heart. They have given themselves over to sensuality, greed, impurity. As Eugene Peterson paraphrases in The Message, "they've lost touch not only with God but with reality. they can't think straight anymore." The world revolves around only themselves. What a vicious, addictive self-destructive cycle we were in. *But* no longer.

b. The New Kingdom: Now We Waltz Together — Eph 4:20-24

I love the "buts" in the Bible. in Ephesians 2, when we were helpless and hopeless, but God. Now, in the contrast to the old way of life as a pagan, Paul says *but* you, *but* now, *but* that's not how you learned Christ.

this "learn Christ" is not just a catechism checklist; it embraces a whole head/heart intimate knowledge and "therefore" kind of discipleship.

The walk turns into a three-step waltz here. Repent, believe, fight. See if you can see it in Paul's imperative commands, the two aorist middle-voice commands and the continuous present passive command sandwiched in-between. Like two concrete slabs of statements with the overflowing, ongoing fountain flowing between.

First, put off, cast off, rid oneself of: *repent.*

Second, be continually renewed: *believe.*

Remember. This is in the present passive voice. It's something you continually passively receive; it is being done to the spirit of your mind by the Spirit. The battle is primarily in your mind. Battle with Scripture to renew your mind.

Third, clothe yourself, put on the new man: *fight.*

It is the truth of Romans 6, where we are dead to sin and alive to righteousness. We are now response-able, because of the indwelling Spirit, to put on the new man. Paul states the truth that we are created after the image of God in true righteousness and holiness. (4:24)

Walk/waltz. Too many Christians do the bunny hop. For me it usually is repent, repent, repent. For others, it may be the exhausting self-focused do, do, do or fight, fight, fight. Some do that Texas two-step of repent/fight. Most of us leave off the believe step. As you are living in the now-not-yet kingdom in that intersection of romans 6-7-8, where you are dead to sin, yet still struggle with it, the biggest fight you have is to keep on believing. Paul is calling us to "be/live" because we are "be/loved." That you believe who you really are: Created to be like God in true righteousness and holiness. In the image of Jesus Christ. Being renewed in the spirit of our minds by the Holy Spirit.

When I hear "put on," I think of playing dress up. Have you ever seen little girls rummage through a dress-up box of beautiful dresses, stick on over their torn jeans? For little boys, pulling on the spiderman outfit with dirty tennis shoes sticking out underneath? I remember when our son, Winn got fitted for a tuxedo for the prom. We went right after track practice and they fit the jacket over his smelly clothes. We looked in the mirror. Not too sure. It wasn't until the night of the prom, when he had taken off the old stuff, showered, and put on the full tuxedo, that he looked like who he was. That's why the first step is to take off.

The mirror is often the worse enemy for us as we try to believe who we really are. All we can see is who we were, our sin, the cinders on our face. It's like the anorexics who struggle with body dysmorphia. What do you see when you look in the mirror? Satan desires to deceive you. We struggle with the real tension that we are in the now-not-yet kingdom, that we are both saint and sinner. How do we integrate these two concepts? Ultimately, we will rest in the mystery of being in Christ. We will be like him in true righteousness and holiness.

II. Holy Ever After — Eph 4:25-5:21
Life in the Now-Not-Yet Kingdom

Paul shows the Ephesians who they are individually (beloved children) and corporately (the church, the body of believers). It is through the church that God will display his wisdom (3:10) and grace to the heavenly realms. "These chapters are a stirring summons to the unity and purity of the church; but they are more than that. Their theme is the integration of the Christian experience (what we are), Christian theology (what we believe) and Christian ethics (how we behave). …what we are governs how we think, and how we think determines how we act." (John Stott) As you pray for the church, always remember to pray for its unity (expressed in love) and purity.

a. Live Loved Together — Eph 4:25-5:2

Ephesians 5:1-2 are "hinge" verses relating to the commands before and after (4:25-32, 5:3-21) and a theme for all of Ephesians. Our whole journey is to learn how to "live loved." Read backwards from Eph 5:2 to 4:25. Because you are loved sacrificially, you can walk in love (5:2). Because you are a beloved child of god, you can imitate him (5:1). Because you are forever and fully forgiven, you can forgive and be kind (4:32). Because you are indwelt and sealed forever by the very real and personal Holy Spirit (4:30), you can grieve him and be motivated to stop those relational sins (stealing, being bitter and sinfully angry, lying) that tear at the body of Christ.

These commands in Eph 4-5 stop me and have in the past made me beat myself up. Now I want them to give me hope, even in the midst of stumbling. I so often fail with my kids…usually with forgetting my duct tape. I'm a word addict. I want to be a Word addict. I've been in Romans 5-8, meditating on the truth that I have transferred realms. I can obey. I am able to not sin. I long to live who I am becoming. But how do I read these verses without despairing? The battle with sin, especially those of my tongue and my emotions, are so strong. It is so hard to live in the now-not-yet kingdom. Satan is shouting that it is "never, never land." God's Word and God's Spirit tell me that I am his workmanship, his masterpiece, created to be like God in true righteousness and holiness.

You walk together with the Triune God and the rest of his royal family. These are the royal family relational rules. This is body life. Between the do's and don'ts, God graciously answers why.

DO NOT	WHY	DO
lie	members	speak truth (in love)
do not sin in anger	don't give Satan a foothold	be angry if you must settle it quickly
do not steal	share with those in need	work with hands
stop corrosive foul rotten self-destructive talk	give grace to hearers	build up, edify with words
do not grieve holy spirit	sealed for day of redemption be kind	
put away all bitterness, rage anger, shouting, slander, malice	as God freely gave to you	be kind, compassionate forgiving, give freely

Grief=love. To grieve in Greek means to cause pain, severe emotional or mental distress, to offend, insult, sadden, mourn, and cause pain of mind or spirit. (Bauer) This is a picture of a person in loving pain for someone else. He is grieved with the corrosive, self-destructive, body destructive sin we do to ourselves and each other. Eugene Peterson's paraphrase in *The Message* says, "Say only what helps. Each word is a gift. Don't grieve God. Don't break his heart. His Holy Spirit, moving and breathing in you, is the most intimate part of your life, making you fit for himself. Don't take such a gift for granted."

Dr. Robert Smith, Jr. of Beeson Divinity School, says that "grieving the Holy Spirit is stepping when he tells you to stop. Quenching the Spirit (1 Thes. 5:19) is stopping when he tells you to step." The picture I have of grieving the guiding Holy Spirit is a gentle touch on the shoulder, his voice behind me telling me which way to walk, and I put my finger up and say, "Let me just say one more thing and then I'll stop." The great comfort is that grieving does not break your sealing in the Spirit. Although sin breaks God's heart, it does not, because of Christ, break his relationship with you. The biblical image of sealing is that of sealing for delivery or certifying of authenticity. It is a picture a loving parent gripping and not letting go of the hand of a rebellious child. *If the Lord delights in a man's way, he makes his steps firm; though he stumbles, he will not fall, for the Lord upholds him with his hand.* (Ps. 37:23-24). The motivation for holy living is love.

Sing the truth of the hymn "O Love that Will Not Let Me Go."

O love that wilt not let me go, I rest my weary soul in thee; I give thee back the life I owe, that in thine ocean depths its flow may richer, fuller be.

God calls us to imitate him. He tells us that we are like him in true righteousness and holiness. This is the God who is compassionate and gracious, slow to anger and abounding in love. That is who we're called to become.

A loved child is not afraid of her father. You are a loved, adopted child of the Abba Father.

b. Live in Light — Eph 5:1-14

Just as a loved child is not afraid of her father, a loved child is not afraid to live in the light.

Would you be willing to be exposed? Would you be willing to fail? In verses 1-14, Paul contrasts old and new, darkness and light, and tells us to live in the light. He doesn't have to go any farther than our tongues. High standards. Foolish, crude talk. Warnings again about God's holiness and our tongues. Difference between love and lust. Sacrifice vs. self-indulgence.

Light is life. Light is power. Light is scary. It exposes. But if you truly believe you are a loved child, you won't be afraid of the light. Pray to get to the point where you want God to expose you, your sin as you look into his loving eyes. You, God, have known this all along. You've wanted me to see it and turn from it. No condemnation.

Light also exposes others. Others may take offense. Choose to still live in the light.

Choose an area you've hidden and allow God to expose it to the light. Instead of hiding or kicking yourself, imagine yourself looking in your Abba's eyes: God, you've known this and wanted me to know it. You want to change me. You love me.

If you are a dearly loved child, and you know your eternal future and your purpose here on earth, and know that you will not fail but you still must fight. You will live with passion and purpose.

Live wisely. Live intentionally. Live with purpose and passion. Don't get caught up in the trivial but understand what the Lord's will is. That means that we can grasp the Lord's will: his revealed will is found in the Bible. For your life, the specifics may seem like a mystery, but you know his "general" will. The rest is by faith, stepping out in the fog.

Don't be drunk but be filled with the Spirit. How can you be filled? Col. 3 is a parallel passage which is very helpful. Let the word of Christ dwell in you richly. Be filled with Spirit is linked to his Word.

Living as a loved child, living in the light unafraid: "We must never separate the Spirit and the Word. To obey the Word and to surrender to the Spirit are virtually identical." This command is in present continuous tense. "We have been 'sealed' with the Spirit once and for all; we need to be filled with the

Spirit and go on being filled with the Spirit every day and every moment of the day." (John Stott)

A practical and supernatural application of these verses is to wake each morning with this prayer, "Lord, fill me with your Holy Spirit" before you rise from bed and then continue asking throughout the day.

Close with a movie clip from *Blood Diamond*.

https://www.youtube.com/watch?v=RZgekp-vQJU

Set in Africa, a young boy is kidnapped by militia and forced to do awful things. They reprogram him so he is too shamed to consider going back to his old life. He is alienated, callous, hard hearted. But his father, Solomon, follows him for a year, pursues him to rescue and redeem him. Watch this scene to truly understand the extend of a father's love that will not let you go.

How would you live differently if you really believed you were loved like that? I am your father and I love you. I sent my Son to die for you. You are mine forever

You do not walk alone. You walk hand in hand with our Triune God. You walk in love holding your Abba Father's hand who will not let you fall when you stumble. You walk holding the Savior's nail-scarred hand. You walk with the sealing grip of the Holy Spirit on your life.

O love that will not let me go.

Believe that you are becoming more and more like God. The now-not-yet kingdom will become the holy-ever-after kingdom. Enchanted. Supernatural. No evil stepmothers. No sin. You will walk in love with one another and with our Triune God. You will live happily and holy ever after.

Week 9: *Live the "Royal Life" Relationally*
Ephesians 5:21-6:9

Where in your key relationships (marriage, parenting, work/school) do you need to submit, respect, love, lead, and/or serve "as to the Lord?"

Nothing like relationships to get us waltzing!
Last week we talked about the Cinderella Syndrome. Taking off the old rags, being made new in our minds, and putting on the new, the new gown, seated on the throne with the Prince…living happily and holy ever after.

Let's look in on Cinderella and Prince Charming on their 10th anniversary. Let's cast Prince Charming not as Jesus, but an ordinary man. Imagine the scene: tv remote, receding hairline, in royal underwear, with high need for naps when there's kingdom work to be done. Just a man with questions, fears, struggles, worries, distractions. But your Prince Charming. Jesus has put you both on the throne to rule with him. He has given you the challenge and the resources to show the heavenly realms a window into God's wisdom and grace by being an image of Christ and the church. You've got three children running around messing up your beautiful castle, and you can't get rid of your stepmother and stepsisters, and the queen mother and king father, because they're family.

How will you respond to Paul's challenge to submit as to the Lord, to respect, to honor, to serve with your whole heart? Great! Now I have to prove myself or great! I get to be who I was meant to be: royalty, a beloved son or daughter. Talk about having to waltz! Repent, believe, fight. Talk about battling the Lie Guy.

Submission: Living a life of personal sacrifice for someone else. One definition of God's will is the doing the next thing I least want to do. We are not to be demanding princesses, pouting princesses, but poured-out princesses. Are you willing to let your life be an offering for your spouse and family, out of reverence to the Lord?

You could be reading this whole section of Scripture saying "but God" focused on the what ifs, past failures, fears for future, confusion and pain, anger, bitterness. Or you could be focused on "but God" that we saw in Ephesians 2. But God, while you were dead made you alive in Christ. Wow! Ultimately our earthly relationships are based on our relationship with the Triune God: our Abba Father, our Lord Jesus Christ, the Holy Spirit.

Do you know you're loved? Alive? Given a life of purpose? Do you trust your Abba Father? Do you desire to reverence the Lord? Are you filled with the Spirit?

Let's look at these verses with an Ephesians 2 "but God" attitude.

Start with Scriptural context:

Why Paul starts with Ephesians 1-3, and with prayer

First go backward. Key hinge verses: Eph 5:21/submit to one another out of reverence to the Lord. Inclusion with 5:33/respect. Ephesians 5:21 is the end of one of Paul's long sentences beginning in vs 18. Be filled with Spirit with the specific actions (addressing in psalms, making melody in heart, giving thanks, submitting) and these are participles dependent on vs. 15's call to walk wisely. Ephesians 5:21 is a hinge verse connecting what is above with what follows. Look back at 5:1-2: another hinge verse to the full call to be who we are meant to be: walk in love, imitate God, sacrificially love like Christ. This is the context of Ephesians 5:21-6:9. Then review Ephesians 1-3: 1-14 who you are in Christ, every spiritual blessing, what God has done for you in Christ. The heartbeat is "in Christ." Vs. 10 is the purpose of the book of Ephesians: that everything will make sense in Christ, that everything in heaven and earth will be drawn together, fit together like a beautiful masterpiece, puzzle, under the headship of Jesus Christ. Then Paul's prayer for enlightenment that we'd see who we really are and what we have in Christ.

Ephesians 2-3 But you...but God...by grace...reveals our purpose individually and corporately. Masterpieces together. As the church. Then Paul prays for empowerment, that we'd be rooted and grounded in love, enabled and living in his power to live the so much more life. Then in Ephesians 4-6 he lays out what the "so much more life" is in our personal relationships, in our walks, and now where it hits home: our marriages, our parenting, and our work. Keep reviewing Ephesians 1-3, especially Paul's prayers as you live out who you really are.

Historical context: Why what Paul is writing is so radical
In the intersection of Hebrew, Greek and Roman culture of 50 AD, Paul's writing was radical. Wives, children, and slaves had no rights and were considered property or tools for the husbands, fathers, and masters. In Greek and Roman culture, wives provided the legitimate heirs but there was no concept of "focus on the family" at that time. Some Hebrew sects could easily divorce their wives for a bad meal or even bad hair day. Children in the Roman Empire who weren't healthy or perfect were discarded. Fathers could sell them into slavery, work them as they wished, and punish them, even to the death penalty. Slaves accounted for about a third of the population in the Roman Empire with estimates of up to 60 million slaves. Most commentators believe that slavery was not as heinous in Paul's day as in our own country's past, with slaves often having incomes and even owning other slaves and regularly being freed after five years. Fifty percent of slaves were freed by the age of 30. For Paul to call men to such a high calling to love and cherish their wives, sacrificing for them; to bring their children up tenderly and in godly instruction; and to treat their servants as they wanted to be treated was groundbreaking. On the

other side of the 20th century, these verses may seem radical because of the countercultural derision of wives submitting, children obeying, and "slaves" accepting their position and serving wholeheartedly. This is the radical nature of God's new society, his "royal" family, his church displaying the mystery of what it means to be "in Christ" and *as to Christ* which is the heartbeat of each of these three relational calls.

I. Marriage and that "S" Word — Eph 5:21-33

It begins with mutual submission. The emphasis is reverencing the Lord in your relationships. We're going from "in Christ" to "as to Christ, for the Lord."

Note: Husbands have 3x as many words of instructions as women in these verses. The heat is really on them. But, let's start with wife's role.

Submission: *Hypotassamai* is the humble recognition of the divine ordering of society. To arrange and order your life for someone else's benefit. Voluntary, free, joyful and thankful partnership, as the analogy of the relationship of the church to Christ shows.

"The verb 'submit, be subordinate' can be used of Christ's submission to the authority of the Father (1 Cor. 15:28) shows it can denote a functional subordination without implying inferiority, or less honor and glory." (Peter O'Brien) Submission turns into an act of worship *out of reverence for the Lord*.

Headship denotes authority and leadership and, as seen in the call to husbands, this headship is that of a servant leader, one who loves sacrificially, unselfishly, and handles the role "with great humility and dependence on the lord, realizing his fallibility and responsibility." (Kent Hughes) Because we do not live in a fairy tale but on a supernatural battlefield and in a fallen world, submission and headship have often been manipulated by both men and women.

Read Genesis 3:16ff. Women will have pain in childbearing. In Hebrew it actually denotes pain from conception on, a constant pain (not shared to same degree by husband) over the raising of children, through adulthood. This toxic combination of desire for control and unending pain often causes pain for the husband.

Men are cursed by futility at work. This often results in a passivity and detachment or distraction to other less painful pursuits.

Best illustration is from *My Big Fat Greek Wedding* where the mother says that the father may be the head of the house, but "she is the neck."

Paul sums up his marital standards in 5:33 where men are to love their wives and wives are to respect (same root word as reverence) their husbands. A wife who communicates respect for her husband in and out of the home, through her words, "nonverbals," and actions, is reverencing the Lord and building up her husband for his role as her sacrificial lover.

Paul's call to husbands (5:25-33) to love, lead, and cherish their wives as Christ loves and serves the church, holds high the view of both marriage and the church. "He sees the marriage relationship as a beautiful model of the church's union in and with Christ. . . . the love he has in mind for the husband sacrifices and serves with a view to enabling his wife to become what God intends her to be. So, the 'submission' and 'respect' he asks of the wife express her response to his love and her desire that he too will become what God intends him to be in his 'leadership.'" (John Stott) These verses also speak of completion. There's a line in the movie *Jerry Maguire* where his new wife Dorothy says, "I love him for the man he wants to be. And I love him for the man he almost is." Jerry simply says to her, "You complete me." The scriptwriter got the heart of a partnership marriage, where a wife sees and calls out what her husband can be and the man (unless gifted for celibacy), is "incomplete—incapable of realizing the divine potential God intends for him in this life—apart from the ministry of his wife in his marriage." (Bryan Chapell) As wives, we are not to abdicate our gifts, intellect, and responsibilities. We are called to the *so much more life* (3:21) that involve challenging another with the insights that God has. Instead of being a silent, submissive, suffering servant, you are called to to be your husband's helpmeet, his ezer, his ally in battle. Another movie illustration: *Fellowship of the Ring*. Arwen the elf princess and Aragorn, the crown prince, are betrothed to each other. When Frodo was mortally wounded by the wraiths, Arwen was the one who could ride faster, and Aragorn agreed. We're partners together in kingdom work.

Some practical advice from the "don't do as Nancy file:"

Prayer: if your husband is responsible for presenting you holy and radiant, let him know how to pray for your heart and walk and your struggles. Ask how to pray for him. It's not always about the kids. Don't have expectations of the length or holy structure. Just pray.

Thanks: Express your gratitude to your husband, often and specifically, until it becomes habit.

Speak well of him to others. Don't badtalk or ridicule him. Sitcoms are not funny at home. There is no laugh soundtrack in real life. Beware of teasing or sarcasm. They rarely create a kind home environment.

Receive his affirmations and believe them. Don't badtalk yourself. Help him to help you.

Guide him to love you well. It took me more than 20 years of marriage to realize that Bill didn't magically know what I want. I had to give up the romantic notion he'd just "know" and I had to train him.

Stop comparing. Look up to the Lord, not around at others.

Battle the curse of futility. See him well. Remind him that he does have what it takes and he is making a difference. At a certain point, Bill was so discouraged by work, all he had was me and the kids. He needed to know that no matter what, I respected him.

II. Parenting and "Childrening" — Eph 6:1-4

Why does God give so few verses on parenting when we need to know the rules?

The Bible is not a parenting manual; it is not a self-help manual. It is a life. Not formula, not techniques. Thank God.

We are all unique, given much freedom within the four verses given here.

Simply, the goal is real, loving relationship with the Triune God that we first have and then radiate to our kids. Goal is to train them in the same basics that we are learning: who we are in

Christ, how much we are loved. My goal for my children: that they love themselves and others like Jesus loves them. Be all they can be in Christ.

Children are to obey and honor their parents. Fathers (the Greek can include mothers) are to bring children up or as John Calvin translated "let them be kindly cherished" and not provoke them to anger. Rear them with tenderness.

Obedience literally means to *listen under* and be should be consistent with God's Word.

Honor means to "acknowledge the parents' God-given authority, and so give them not only our obedience, but our love and respect as well." (John Stott) As adult children, we never outgrow our obligation to honor and respect our parents, especially in a culture that often forgets and neglects the elderly. As parents, we are not to "goad our children to resentment." There is a call for consistent discipline but never with sarcasm, harshness, shaming, or manipulation. When we see and value each child as a gift and unique "masterpiece," we are using our roles to tenderly shape them to their God-given potential. Almost nothing causes a child's personality to blossom and gifts to develop like the positive encouragement of loving, understanding parents. Just as we are not to abdicate our roles as husbands and wives, we are not to abdicate our roles as parents in the hard job of consistent discipline, training, and instruction of our children with the goal of knowing and following the Lord.

Practical suggestions:
Stop comparison shopping. it is unto the Lord, not unto a cookie cutter standard of other Christians. My kids are so unique. Stick with the few verses in Scripture and pray and seek counsel and have fun.

Stop parenting out of pride. I repent of the fear I had of what other parents would say about me, not with the primary motivation that they will be gently guided into the nurture and admonition of the Lord. I always had Barney Fife from Andy Griffith show in my head saying "you gotta nip it in the bud."

For younger kids: Slow down. I read from a child development specialist that we don't let our kids tie their shoes; we use Velcro. We don't let kids get in their car seats; we put them in. We're rushing all the time. I repent that I was so harsh over self-imposed activities and deadlines.

See and enjoy them as unique gifts. Be respectful of them as well. Try not to shame, guilt, or manipulate them to obedience. The tough, slow, consistent, stumbling, by faith job of just keeping at the basics.

Speak well of them in front of others. Affirm them. Thank them.

Discipline them. Narrow the list down to the essentials which will point to Christ and give them freedom. Someone did a survey of third-generation Christians to see what it was that helped them keep their faith and the answer surprised the surveyors. They said it was having a fun home. It's not just about the daily devotions.

Give them something bigger. Introduce mission trips, soup kitchens, your life interacting with those in need.

Most important thing is your own relationship with the Lord. That's how they learn.

III. Working Relationships — Eph 6:5-9

Sincerely means singled heartedness and the single focus is *as to the Lord*. Conscientiously means whether anyone is looking or not. Pleasantly has to do with an attitude of good cheer and building up, not tearing down. The call for masters (or employers or supervisors) is to live by the Golden Rule and so treat their workers with respect, sincerity, consistency, and a good working environment. "Paul does not condone the system of slavery but instead provides instructions to believing masters and slaves regarding their relationship to each other in the Lord, and how this should be lived out within the bounds of their social and legal culture. The result, as is often observed, is that slavery slowly died out in antiquity through the influence of Christianity." (ESV Study Bible notes)

Conclusion

Do you know how much God loves you? Do you know God's ultimate purpose for his kingdom and for your life? How will you live out mutual submission? Will you submit first to being filled with the Spirit, so you supernaturally are able to live full-out for your husband, love and train your children, that you are continually able to fit under the headship of Christ?

Let's pray:

Oh Abba Father, for many this section of Scripture is filled with pain and confusion. We are saying "but God" in relation to our relationships. Please help us to remember the ultimate "but God" on what you have done for us in Christ. Help us to relish the roles you've given us as wives/husbands, mothers/fathers, daughters/sons, workers and friends. Realizing that you will get the glory as we live full-out a life of love like Christ. For those waiting to be wives and mothers or workers, please fulfill their deepest desires. For those in difficult marriages, for those with parenting struggles, with prodigal children, we ask you to give us more than we ask or think. We can't do it, but we believe your Word that says you will do it through us and in us. Help us to continue to dance with you.

Week 10: *A Call to Arms and Prayer*
Ephesians 6:10-24

Are you aware and prepared for the very real spiritual battle you are in?

Be prepared. You're up against far more than you can handle on your own. Take all the help you can get, every weapon God has issued, so that when it's all over but the shouting you'll still be on your feet. Truth, righteousness, peace, faith, and salvation are more than words. Learn how to apply them. You'll need them throughout your life. God's word is an indispensable weapon. In the same way, prayer is essential in this ongoing warfare. Pray hard and long. Pray for your brothers and sisters. Keep your eyes open. Keep each other's spirits up so that no one falls behind or drops out. Eph. 6:13-18 The Message

It's a war out there

Three keys to the battle Ephesians 6:10-24
We've spent the last 10 weeks focused on who we are in Christ and how we are to live that out. We are adopted sons and daughters of the King. We are loved, powerful, poured-out masterpieces with a purpose: to be to the praise of the glory of God, that God will bring all things under the headship of Christ. This week, we are going to focus on the truth that we are called to arms. That is scary to me. I go to any length to avoid conflict or discomfort.

As we look at these verses: Realize the reality and intensity of the war that we're in.

How do you view the world? Does it feel like an assembly or carpool line broken up with trips to the amusement park or dips in the hot tub? Do you think of life as more as a cruise ship or a battleship? If life is a battle, do you find yourself a soldier, part of the USO entertainment troop, the refreshment crew, a doctor on the mash unit, or a war correspondent? I often realize it's a spiritual battle but feel like I'm watching it on CNN. Ephesians 6:10-24 is a practical spiritual warfare manual that is puzzling to read for those who wonder, "What would Satan want with me? I'm of no significance." It is disturbing for those who battle even thinking God still works "supernaturally." It is uncomfortable for those who enjoy life on the comfortable safe sidelines.

The keys which Paul is giving us is: Be aware! Be prepared! Pray!

Movie clip: Aragon speaking to Eowyn in The Two Towers

https://www.youtube.com/watch?v=Wpk4VqGO_Us

You are a daughter of the king. What is it you fear?

First: Acknowledge there is a battle and you're in it.

Second: Make the choice between the comfortable life and the called-out life.

A life of purpose, significance, that counts for Christ. We long for it. We fear it. Takes faith. You will get noticed by the Enemy. But rejoice, you are on the winning side. And it's not your battle. It is the risen Lord Jesus Christ who has won the war. But we are still in the battle.

I. Awareness — Ephesians 6:10-12

Know you're in a non-stop battle.
This was a hard truth for me. I want an occasional skirmish with as much hot tub time as possible. But we must be ever vigilant, ever on guard. Like fighting terrorism. The Lie Guy would like nothing better for you to be comfortable on the sidelines in the fog. And our role is not to be on the cheerleading, entertainment, or refreshment committee. All believers are warriors.

Know your strength (the Lord).
Finally, be strong in the Lord. What simple words. Be strong. Another passive imperative. Be strengthened in. In the Lord. Theme of Ephesians is "in Christ together." Not in yourself by yourself. Think about facing the school yard bully alone. Taunting, teasing, pushing. Now change the picture. How would you feel if your daddy or big brother were standing behind you as you faced your Enemy? Your attitude would change. You know you're puny. You know your father is powerful. Oh, to have eyes to see.

2 Kings 6:15-17 When the servant of the man of God got up and went out early the next morning, an army with horses and chariots had surrounded the city. "Oh my Lord, what shall we do?" The servant asked. "Don't be afraid," the prophet answered. "Those who are with us are more than those who are with them." And Elisha prayed, "O Lord open his eyes so he may see." Then the Lord opened the servant's eyes, and he looked and saw the hills full of horses and chariots of fire all around Elisha.

Know your enemy.
Satan is real, active and alive on our planet. Powerful, wicked, cunning, a bully and beguiler. Intimidator and insinuator. Force and fraud. He is at his wiliest when he persuades people he does not exist.

In *Screwtape Letters*, C. S. Lewis, writes, "There are two equal and opposite errors into which our race can fall about the devils. One is to disbelieve in their existence. The other is to believe, and to feel an excessive and unhealthy interest in them."

Screwtape Letters and *Perelandra* are good books that give you a picture of Satan's tactics.

Satan is a being. He is subtle and strategic. Not omnipotent or omnipresent. Does have a league of his own. Not a force, not an institution. Not a book. Not flesh and blood. That means although he can use those things, that's not where your battle is. Your spouse, your boss, your child, your parent, your school system, your government, the movie industry is not your enemy. Satan is your enemy.

Attack warnings: Can be any/all of these: Afflicted, success, idleness, isolated, dying, tired, discouraged.

How can we expect to stand against the assaults of such enemies? It is impossible. We are far too weak and too ingenuous. Yet many—if not most—of our failures and defeats are due to our foolish self-confidence when we either disbelieve or forget how formidable our spiritual enemies are. Only the power of God can defend and deliver us from the might, the evil and the craft of the devil. . . It is his power which raised Jesus Christ from the dead and enthroned him in the heavenly places, and which has raised us from the death of sin and enthroned us with Christ." (John Stott)

Satan does not want you to be prepared for the battle. Awareness is such a key. Have you been wanting to pray more, reach out to your neighbors, answer a call to lead at church? And unusual amounts of things are going wrong? Have you ever thought you're getting attention from the Enemy? Sometimes we have such a poor view of our own walk that we don't realize that we're having an impact for God's kingdom. It is a humbling experience to realize that you've been noticed.

II. Preparedness — Ephesians 6:13-17

Know your weaknesses/resources.
Warriors not only knows the Enemy but knows themselves, their strengths and weaknesses.

Paul talks about armor because he knows his own and your weaknesses. Think of the armor as different ways of saying Jesus! And the resources he provides you. Eph 1:3 all spiritual blessings in Christ are ours. Paul says to put on the full armor of God. He never said to take it off, especially at nighttime when there's so much spiritual attack. When you could be struggling with doubts, sorrows, fears. Where are you weak? Let's see where Paul sees our weaknesses and need for god's resources:

Know your resources/weapons.
Paul is chained to a Roman guard day after day, month after month. He can illustrate what is needed in battle by who is seated next to him. The guard provides the best illustration of being a prepared soldier in the battlefield.

Belt of truth: The Roman soldier's belt cinched his tunic and sword in place so he could be ready for battle.

Where are we weak: so easily deceived, so easily believe the Lie Guy.

Resource: Jesus is the truth. The Word belted around us. Always a combination of truth and application: Know the truth. Live the truth out.

Breastplate of righteousness: We're weak in our view of selves and our justification. Resource is breastplate: The breastplate or *thorax* protected the soldiers' vital organs, especially the heart. It is the righteousness of Jesus covering you. Not what you see. Not what Satan sees. What God sees when he sees you: Jesus.

"To have been justified by his grace through simple faith in Christ crucified, to be clothed with a righteousness which is not one's own, but Christ's, to stand before God not condemned but accepted—this is an essential defense against an accusing conscience and against the slanderous attacks of the evil one, whose Hebrew name ('Satan') means 'adversary' and whose Greek title (diabolos, 'devil') means 'slanderer.'"

Footwear: feet fitted with gospel of peace: Where are we weak: Forget the gospel, forget peace. Jesus is our peace. Paul is describing the Roman *caliga* or half-boot, an open-toed leather boot with a heavily nail-studded sole which was tied to the ankles and shins with straps. These were boots not for running but for marching and digging in and taking a stand. Like football cleats. These sandal-boots gave the foot traction and prevented sliding. These boots were digging into the gospel of peace. The boots are both peace *with* God (Romans 5:1) and the peace *of* God (John 14:27)—*shalom*. Where there had been enmity with God, there is now peace, well-being, and a sense of his presence. (Kent Hughes)

Shield of faith: Where we're weak: We are so easily caught by Satan's fiery darts. Jesus is our shield. He has taken all the fiery darts of both Satan and the wrath of God. We live by faith in him. The Roman soldier's shield or *scotum* was the size of a small door which could cover his whole body and was made of leather, wood and metal, and often soaked in water to quench the flames of the burning arrows sent by the enemy. Often they held them up as a line as they moved forward. See it in community. We help each other as we hold out our shields of faith against the fiery darts. We can deflect them from others as well.

Fiery darts: Customized to your weak areas: discouragement, doubt, fear, despair, anger,

The enemy sends accusations, false guilts, "unsought thoughts of doubt and disobedience, rebellion, lust, malice or fear. . . (but) God himself 'is a shield to those who take refuge in him (Prov. 30:5), and it is by faith that we flee to him for refuge. For faith lays hold of the promises of god in times of doubt and depression, and faith lays hold of the power of God in times of temptation." (John Stott) What customized darts are being sent your way? How are you shielded in God's word and promises by faith?

Helmet of salvation: Where we're weak: Our minds, assurance, doubts. This is where I need the most protection my mind. Roman soldiers took helmets seriously. They were heavy, usually of bronze, and covered most of the head, cheek, and neck. It would take a hammer or axe to penetrate the *cassis*. The 'helmet of salvation' is the assurance of salvation and the resulting confidence it brings. (Kent Hughes) Salvation must be seen in past, present, and future terms, it assures us of future and final salvation in Heaven where we will receive our inheritance and be the inheritance of the Lord.

Sword of the Spirit: Which is the Word of God the Bible. Our weakness: We don't know his truth or believe it. The sword refers to the *machaira*, the doubled-edged short sword that Roman soldiers used in hand-to-hand combat. It is the offensive weapon (along with prayer). Jesus is the Word. Look at how Satan attacked Jesus in the desert and his defense: Jesus knew the Word of God and spoke it and Satan had to leave. Oh, that we would be biblical thinkers.

Luther's hymn: One little word shall fell him. Our skill with the blade is proportional to time spent in Word.

How can we increase our "sword skills?" By reading, meditating, memorizing and studying the Scripture. Consider reading through the Bible on a regular basis. Soak in specific passages and memorize key verses and wrestle with understanding the whole redemptive thread of Scripture and the meaning and application to your life.

Know your position.
Dead, raised, seated, kneeling, walking, finally standing (stated 3 times).

When you've done everything, stand. It sounds simple. It is everything. In fierce storms seamen tell us that we must put the ship in a certain position and keep her there. Sometimes, like Paul, "when you can see neither sun nor stars and no small tempest lies on you; and then you can do but one thing, there is only one way. Reason cannot help you; past experiences give you no light. Even prayer fetches no consolation. Only a single course is left. You must put your soul in one position and keep it there. You must stay upon the Lord; and come what may—winds, waves, cross-seas, thunder, lightning, frowning rocks, roaring breakers—no matter what, you must lash yourself to the helm, and hold fast your confidence in God's faithfulness, his covenant engagement, his everlasting love in Christ Jesus. Lash yourself to his cross."

Richard Fuller, Streams in the Desert

European masterpieces: Ulysses tied to the ship's mast as they pass the Sirens.

When you think you can't do anything else, will you stand? Will you be in the Word? Will you pray?

III. Prayer — Ephesians 6:18-24

Prayer is so important that Paul drops all armor metaphor and simply says "Pray!" Prayer is to be the breath behind all our spiritual warfare and weapons (note Paul stresses *all* four times in exhortation to pray). It is the second offensive weapon in our arsenal. "Scripture and prayer belong together as the two chief weapons which the Spirit puts into our hands." (John Stott) Eugene Peterson, the translator of *The Message*, began writing this North American translation of Scripture as a way to get people to pray Scripture. "*Scriptureprayer*, or *prayerscripture*. It is this fusion of God speaking to us (Scripture) and our speaking to him (prayer) that the Holy Spirit uses to form the life of Christ in us." We are in a cosmic spiritual battle... The spiritual weapons of our warfare are: *truth, righteousness, peace, faith, confidence, the word, and prayer*—prayer which *is Spirit-directed* ('pray in the spirit'); *continual* ('on all occasions'); *varied* ('with all kinds of prayers and requests'); *persistent* ('be alert and always keep on praying'); *intercessory* ('for all the saints').

Attitude of prayer: Constantly communicating with, crying out, in the Spirit. Simply crying out over and over again God I can't. You can save me. I believe. Help my unbelief.

Know your objective.
To be to the praise of his glory. To bring all things together in unity under Christ. Live a life of love and light. Remind yourself of this as Satan distracts you and tries to get you to fight the wrong battles. Not for performance, not for appearances. True battle of faith, love, glory to God as we love one another. Live in unity.

Know the ending.
That's what will make you courageous, not fearful. The war is won. We still must stand and pray. Scene from the *Two Towers*, where Pippin and Gandalf are in the midst of the battle and Merry is losing courage and afraid to die. Gandalf says "That is not the end, don't you know? There's a far green country." He begins to describe it and Pippin says, "That's not so bad."

https://www.youtube.com/watch?v=r-odIIQORQ4

Do you pray and ask for prayer for yourself? Why not? Lie Guy says you're not important enough, he doesn't you to reveal fear or weakness.

If you are grasping who you are in Christ, seated with him, standing with him, praying, you will still feel the heat of the battle. You will be tired. You will also experience living a life fille with purpose, significance and power. A life not of trivial things but a life of love and light where you do make a difference.

Week 11: *LOL: Living Out Loud*
Review of Ephesians

I encourage you to review the final weekly lesson questions and allow the participants to tell which parts of Ephesians most resonate with them and why.

Which of the "buts" of Ephesians stand out most for you?

Show completed puzzle (beautiful Heaven like scene or picture of Jesus?)

Your puzzle piece will help reveal Jesus Christ to a watching world and heavenly realm.

Live a life that glorifies God and inspires holy envy (from the angels).

How will you believe what is true and already true? How will you fight the Lie Guy?

Read from *The Silver Chair* C. S. Lewis

Puddleglum's speech in defiance of the the Green Lady (aka the Lie Guy):

Suppose we have only dreamed, or made up, all those things—trees and grass and sun and moon and stars and Aslan himself. Suppose we have. Then all I can say is that, in that case, the made-up things seem a good deal more important than the real ones. Suppose this black pit of a kingdom of yours is the only world. Well, it strikes me as a pretty poor one. And that's a funny thing, when you come to think of it. We're just babies making up a game, if you're right. But four babies playing a game can make a play-world which licks your real world hollow. That's why I'm going to stand by the play world. I'm on Aslan's side even if there isn't any Aslan to lead it. I'm going to live as like a Narnian as I can even if there isn't any Narnia. So, thanking you kindly for our supper, if these two gentlemen and the young lady are ready, we're leaving your court at once and setting out in the dark to spend our lives looking for Overland. Not that our lives will be very long, I should think; but that's a small loss if the world's as dull a place as you say."

www.ingramcontent.com/pod-product-compliance
Lightning Source LLC
Chambersburg PA
CBHW081222020426
42331CB00012B/3068